THIS PLACE IS AWESOME

A Strange Funny Drunken Sad Noisy Week
With The Dreadnoughts

Words and Photos
by Adam PW Smith

This book is being self-published by the author. This book's success depends on people like you. If you enjoy this book, please tell your friends about it. Posting to Facebook, Twitter, or your favourite Web site will ensure that the community of like-minded people grows.

Please feel free to contact me at adam@adampwsmith.com

More contact information for the author can be found at the end of the book.

Thanks
apws

This is the second edition

ISBN 978-1-105-25515-1

For JMSmith,
who put hard work, curiosity, and resourcefulness into my genes.

ACKNOWLEDGEMENTS

Obviously the first thank you needs to go to the band for making room for me in the van. You are like family to me – you're a pain in the ass and it seems like I only ever see most of you once a year these days, but I'll have a cry when you're gone.

My wife, Nancy, provides all manner of support. All sorts of things become possible when you have someone like her in your life.

David allowed me to stay in his spacious and fantastically convenient flat when I was in London, which is unbelievably generous of him.

Kev, Zoey, Jamer and the babber, and all of the people in Bristol went above and beyond when it comes to hospitality and generosity. I reserve a special place in my heart for all of you and the Wilkins Cider Farm too.

Thom deserves special thanks, too, for being a gracious and generous host.

As much I may whinge about the quality of accommodations throughout this book, I am nevertheless grateful to everyone who offered up a couch, blanket, mattress, or patch of floor space. If you ever come to Vancouver give me a ring and I'm sure we can find a spot in the garage and a few newspapers for you.

Iolanda provided significant encouragement and was also responsible for getting me going in the right direction in the crucial early days. Ryan provided some excellent advice and perspective on the publishing industry. Many friends provided encouragement and suggestions to keep this project rolling.

Thanks to Tom and Nardwuar for their contributions. And thanks to all the musicians of the Vancouver indie music scene who put time, effort, money, and inspiration into their work.

THIS PLACE IS AWESOME

A LITTLE BACKGROUND INFORMATION.	1
ALL THE STANDARD INDIGNITIES BUT ONE.	3
WELCOME TO THE TOUR, ADAM.	7
THIS IS WHAT I IMAGINED CANADIANS WERE LIKE.	19
LOOK AT THIS PLACE, IT'S AWESOME.	41
YOU REALLY SHOULD DO SOMETHING ABOUT THE TRAMPS.	59
IS THAT THE BEST YOU CAN DO, YOU PUSSIES?	77
IF YOU COULD GO HOME NOW, WOULD YOU?	95
AM I BEING REWARDED OR PUNISHED?	109
ALL OVER BUT THE SHOWERING.	125
THE RECOVERY.	139
ABOUT THE AUTHOR.	143
IF YOU LIKED THAT, TRY THIS…	145

A LITTLE BACKGROUND INFORMATION.

This is not a description of anyone's personality as a whole. It's a collection of observed behaviours. I've tried to make sense of those behaviour in places, but no one should make the mistake of thinking that they're getting a rounded view of who these people are. Think of it like were looking at a person with rabies. You can observe them foaming at the mouth and look deeper to find the virus that's causing it, but it's hardly an accurate view of who that person is. It just explains why they bit you and then ran away.

The Dreadnoughts are a five-piece band from Vancouver that are doing their best to defy easy description. They started out as a lark – a Celtic punk band with no greater mission than to play some shows and get splendidly drunk. As their reputation for exceptional live shows grew, and a following that insisted on shows lasting until two or three in the morning formed, it became clear that they had a shot at something more.

I first saw The Dreadnoughts in January 2007 at their second ever show. As someone who loves live music and bands that can put on a great show I was immediately drawn to them. Since then I've seen them countless times, photographed their shows thoroughly, and found the bottom of more than a few gin bottles with them. When I found out that they were going to be in Britain for a week in the summer of 2009 I volunteered to come along and photograph the mayhem.

Stories of rock bands on the road are the stuff of legends; we all know the clichés of the young yobs throwing groupies from bed to bed, throwing televisions off of hotel balconies, and throwing up in every corner imaginable. The truth is rarely so colourful or exciting. It is a combination of hard work and fantastically tedious boredom. A living contradiction of moments of hero worship couched by long stretches of lonely anonymity. I've heard that a well known rock icon once said "if the young women who came to our hotel rooms really knew what we wanted they'd bring clean socks a decent meal" (sadly the story turns out to be apocryphal, but the sentiment is not far from the mark). I was hoping to capture something of the real world of touring, as it exists for the 99% of bands who don't tour in private jets and five star hotels.

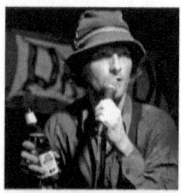 Nick (Uncle Touchy) is the lead singer and guitarist.

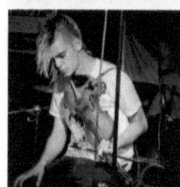 Kyle (Seamus O'Flanahan) plays fiddle and occasionally accordion, and sings backing vocals.

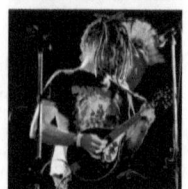 Drew (The Dread Pirate Druzil) plays mandolin and tin whistle, and also contributes backing vocals.

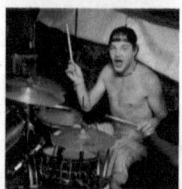 Marco (The Stupid Swedish Bastard) is the drummer.

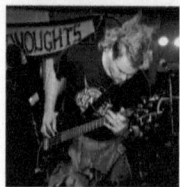 Andrew (Squid Vicious) plays bass.

ALL THE STANDARD INDIGNITIES BUT ONE.

Day Zero
August 20, 2009 – Vancouver

I'm sitting in my home office on a quiet street in Vancouver. Seamus just texted me – his band, The Dreadnoughts are back on Canadian soil. I am both relieved and astonished. I am also, finally, after two months, feeling like I have recovered from the week I spent with them.

I signed on to travel with The Dreadnoughts for the week that they would be touring Britain. I had an inkling of what I was setting myself up for before I left. I've spent almost 30 years of my life hanging around with independent musicians. I've provided a quiet night's accommodations to dozens of bands, from the most obscure and shortlived indie bands to more recognizable names like Skinny Puppy. I've seen small stages from all sides, including underneath. I've been around bands on the verge of collapse from internal conflicts. I've seen people eat things that ought not be eaten. I've seen the things that are supposed to be eaten thrown at a fan in the corner to see how far they'd fly back across the room (I'm looking at you, Grapes of Wrath). I've even done road trips. But I'd never done a proper tour.

As far as I can tell, there was only one standard indignity that I didn't suffer while on tour with The Dreadnoughts. Not that I was alone in suffering. Far from it – I only had to endure the endless, soul-sucking, death by a thousand tiny knives for a week. The level of zen detachment required to survive three months of that hellish existence is beyond me. Or perhaps I'm just too old to put up with that kind of shit.

It's hard to really describe the touring experience as The Dreadnoughts were having it. It's the combination of being constantly busy and yet seldom with anything new or interesting. There is persistent deadline pressure, but so much time is spent waiting for the deadline to arrive. In the end I realised that it's kind of like moving day – every day. A hellish Groundhog Day existence where you get up, put all of your heaviest belongings in a van, drive to a new location, take them out of the van, arrange them, drink some beer and shout a lot, fall asleep in a place that may or may not have a bed – and then do it all again tomorrow. And the next day. And the next day. And do that for three months.

For The Dreadnoughts, the ordeal began some time in May as they drove away from the alley behind their practice space in downtown Vancouver in their newly acquired minivan, bought from a bitter man who was selling it to get some bizarre revenge on his ex-wife and packed to bursting with instruments and merchandise. They drove across Canada, left the van in Toronto, and flew to Europe. They then picked up a different van (described in detail later) and drove it all over Germany, France, Holland, Austria, Switzerland, Poland... it sounds very glamourous. It isn't. There was no tour manager, no merch person, no driver. Just the five physical bodies, and as many personal demons and neuroses as would fit.

Some of them had done extensive tours with other bands, while the others were experiencing serious road life for the first time. Most of the Dreadnought tours up to that point had been three to five day jaunts into the interior of BC, sometimes venturing as far as Alberta. Their reputation in Western Canada was small but very solid. They could be counted on to fill small dive bars well past capacity and keep the entire audience until the wee hours of the morning. Steeped in their personal vision of the "punk ethos" they loved nothing more than getting obscenely sweaty in front of a small group of rabid fans. Far from dreaming of stadiums and first class plane tickets, most members of the band seemed to have a pathological aversion to anything that might be misconstrued as rock star behaviour or treatment. (Years later I would be sitting in an East Van bar listening to one of The Dreadnoughts asking a local punk legend about what the largest crowd they ever played to

This Place Is Awesome

was, and what was the largest number of people you could play to and still consider yourself a "punk band.")

No two Dreadnoughts shows were ever the same. It was a blunderbuss approach to performance - fill the muzzle with a collection of songs, pack it tight with the indiscriminate furious energy of youth, add a bit of alcohol to give it some extra punch, turn towards the audience, and pull the trigger. It never failed to go off. The only question in this case was who would be standing in the way and how they would react to it. Without the support of industrial-strength hype or publicity their ability to make a good impression was down to a combination of unreliable, inconsistent local promoters and luck. An invitation to return was rarely a matter of any concern, but much depended on getting that first crowd out to see an unknown and unheard band.

When I met up with the boys they had already spent five continuous weeks cooped up in the van, driving through places with names that they couldn't pronounce, playing to crowds that had never heard of them, listening to languages they couldn't speak, drinking prodigious quantities of all manner of liquor, and rarely doing laundry. Their performance schedule was impressive by anyone's standards – there was rarely a day off. The band, as a cohesive, compatible unit was getting it's first serious shakedown.

For me it started in Bristol on a sunny day in July.

"I remember when I first saw you in Bristol.
You were shaved and clean and had clean clothes on.
I was so fucking jealous of you."

– Marco

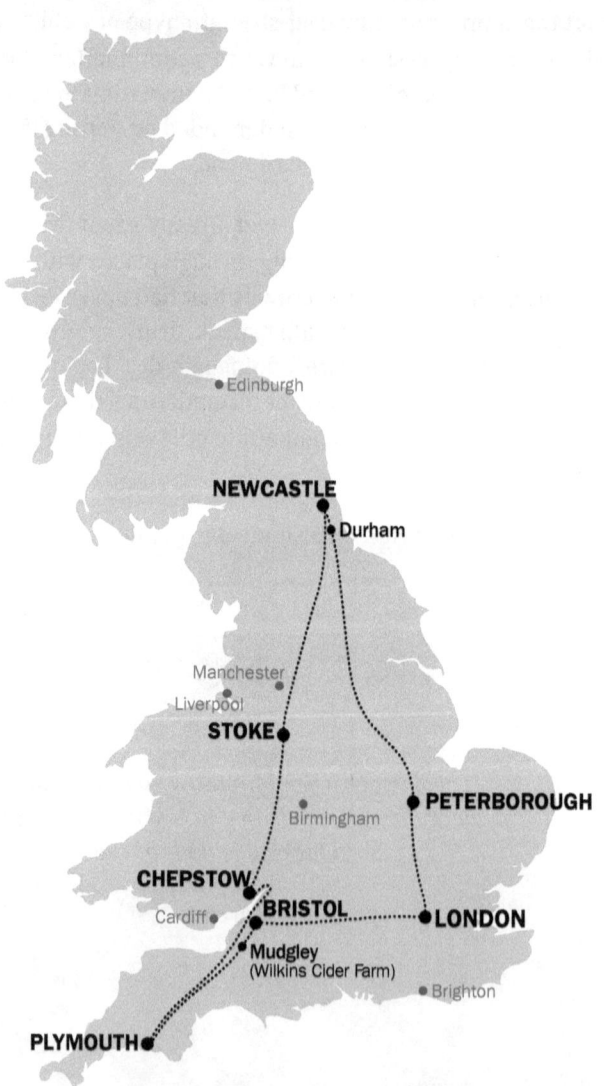

Edinburgh

NEWCASTLE
Durham

Manchester
Liverpool
STOKE

PETERBOROUGH

Birmingham

CHEPSTOW
Cardiff
BRISTOL
LONDON

Mudgley
(Wilkins Cider Farm)

Brighton

PLYMOUTH

This Place Is Awesome

WELCOME TO THE TOUR, ADAM.

Day One
July 1, 2009 – Bristol

"Welcome to the tour" were the final words from Squid Vicious, the bassist, as he fell asleep on the couch some time around 3 A.M., and started to snore with a tone and volume that sounded like a phone book being ripped in half.

I had agreed to meet the boys in Bristol – the capital of cider country and home turf for one their favourite bands, the inexplicably named "Surfin' Turnips." The Turnips play "Cider Punk," a genre of roughly-played music that is, to put it mildly, obsessed with cider. The Dreadnoughts wrote a song about the area called "The West Country" and they cover the Turnips tribute to cider called, in a fit of splendid understatement and efficiency... "Cider" (the lyrics consist of that word alone, repeated over and over). The Dreadnoughts consider this area to be part of their spiritual homeland.

I flew to London, stayed there overnight, and caught the train the next morning to Bristol where I found that evening's venue – The Reckless Engineer – conveniently located at the bottom of the short road that led out of the station. While the government and the private sector slowly dismantle or render unusable elements of the British railroad system, it's still a relatively easy way to get around. As Canadians, we tend to think of traveling by train as a quaint historical artifact – something done as a novelty. But that's because of the impossibly large size of our country. No one here has a week to get from one side of it to the other. In Britain, a cross country journey is typically matter of hours. To go the longest way – from Penzance to the top of Scotland – is less than a full day (an hour shy of a full day, I'm told). Those who have travelled Canada by ground know that it takes a day and a half just to get around Lake Superior.

I hadn't spoken to any of the boys for a few days. It was a matter of faith that they would be at the venue, given that they were coming in from Holland. The sum total of our arrangement was "we'll meet up in Bristol." Planning, with The Dreadnoughts, was always an exercise in minimalism.

I settled into the small pub, which was spartan and utilitarian but clean and decent, and waited. It looked more like a bright, simple, university cafeteria than the traditional dark wood and low ceilings that you might expect from a pub in Britain. But as is clearly evident from the many attempts to create a British-style pub in Canada, a pub is more a state of mind and construct of community than a collection of dinner plates on the wall with pictures of the royal family.

By mid-afternoon the boys had arrived, and so had Jamer from the Surfin' Turnips. It's a strange feeling to be in a foreign and distant location and then have friendly faces from far away suddenly appear. Instead of it being surreal to see those faces in an alien environment, it suddenly changes the previously unnatural location into something familiar and comfortable. For me at least, it's the people (either present in person or as memories) that make me feel like I belong. I went from feeling like the conspicuous outsider in the room, to feeling at home and in my element again.

We spent a short time settling in (and downing a pint) and I gave Seamus the only thing that I was asked to bring from Canada - two cans of "Got2bGlued" hairspray. He had been unable to reliably find a product that would keep his mohawk in shape. We caught our breath and then headed out to find a floating cider barge.

The locals were exactly what someone keen on using a tour to learn a bit about the world would want. They were eager to show us the parts of their world that were significant to them. The floating cider barge was the kind of thing you would only ever find in Bristol; it is literally a barge, moored in a canal, fitted out as a pub and serving at least 30 varieties of local cider. It's imaginatively called "The Apple." West County folk can be charmingly concrete. On this particular sunny and warm summer afternoon the outer deck and adjacent bank were comfortably filled with young people. We settled into the couches of the barge's interior and I caught up with a few stories from the tour to that point.

Having tasted some very fine brews, we headed back to the venue, sidetracked only by the need to drop into another pub. Outside The Seven Stars our hosts took pride in pointing out the plaque on the wall indicating that this was the meeting place for a group of abolitionists in the 18th century. It even has its own Wikipedia page. These days it looks like a pretty standard pub, albeit one where the server bears a startling resemblance to Dave Grohl and hands out Curly Wurly bars to everyone in your party if he likes you.

Back at the venue we ate a decent but unremarkable dinner and the show got underway. It was a small crowd, but they were intensely enthusiastic. The stage was little more than a raised part of the floor that was surely used as another seating area when there were no shows. It was surrounded by a railing that provided a convenient jumping off point for anyone keen on stage diving but stymied by the fact that getting enough height from the "stage" to land on top of the crowd would require jumping at least six feet up in the air first. Two opening bands got the evening rolling with variations on the punk sound. The second band, a duo of guitar and drums, threw toilet paper rolls into the audience and started a process that soon left the entire stage and half the audience covered in toilet paper streamers. It was surprisingly entertaining.

The Dreadnoughts turned in a spirited show, beset with standard technical issues. The PA was dodgy and Nick's guitar strap broke, necessitating a hasty fix using gaff tape and a lot of nervous hope. The Surfin Turnips were the last official band on the bill. Most of their hugely entertaining show was accompanied by a band member who's job involved dressing in various costumes and masks and performing rites that left me completely confused and inexplicably amused. At one point he wore a trenchcoat and a rubber mask that looked like a giant sea anemone had attacked his face, and then played a kalimba. I haven't the faintest idea what the joke was, but I respect anyone who is willing to put that much thought and effort into a performance. I'm sure it was hysterically funny to the locals. After all the bands had played, Marco the drummer decided he wasn't done yet. Seamus and Andrew joined him and thus was born "Seamus and the Cider Riders."

For the uninitiated, the "rider" is the name given to the document many bands submit when they book a show that lists all the things they need in the way of food, drinks, and other necessities. Sometimes the drinks part is the longest and most specific. A "cider rider" would be the part of the documentation that lists how much and what kind of cider will be required for the band to perform. The Dreadnoughts were not yet at the stage where they could be that specific and demanding. They had to content themselves with making humourous references for the time being.

Seamus and The Cider Riders stumbled through a few attempts at Guns of Brixton, Blitzkrieg Bop, and Too Drunk To Fuck. When the excess energy finally started to wane, many hours after the first chord of the evening had been struck, they gave up the ghost and went back to drinking.

Eventually we loaded up the van and headed into a dark part of Bristol to find our lodgings for the night. Our hosts Zoey and Kev lived in a cozy, character-filled house filled with comfortable furniture and room to relax. They were beyond hospitable and I was lulled into a false sense of security. Sure I was sleeping on the floor, but that was not a new experience for me and Zoey repeatedly insisted that I "take some comfort" in the form of blankets and pillows. The house was quiet, clean, and comfortable. It was probably the last house I would find in this condition until I returned to London.

Fate placed me carefully on the tee with a nice view of the fairway the next day. I completely failed to see the club that was about to knock me senseless across the country.

This Place Is Awesome

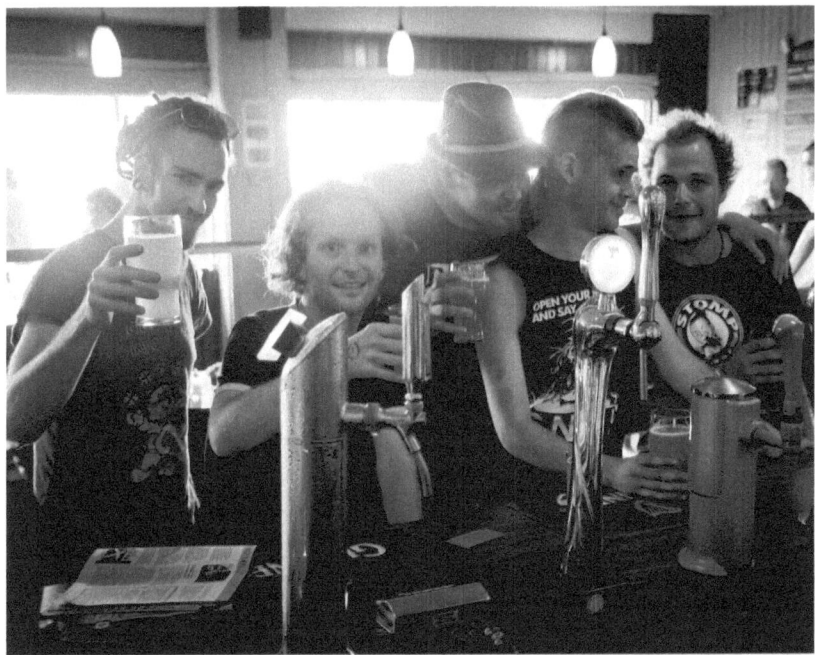

The Dreadnoughts arrive at the Reckless Engineer in Bristol, fresh off the boat from Holland. Well.. perhaps "fresh" is a poor choice of words. "Recently" off the boat from Holland. From left to right, Drew, Nick, Andrew, Seamus, and Marco.

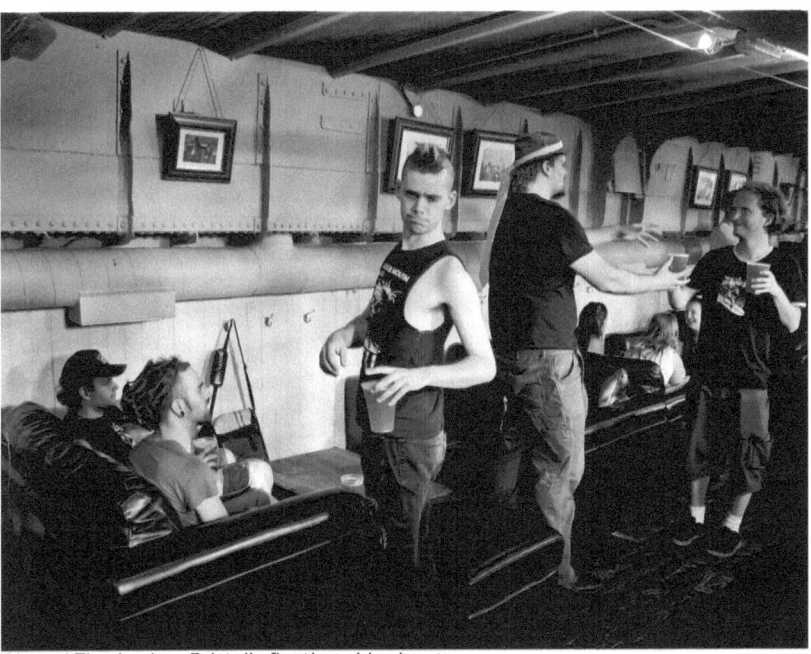

Aboard The Apple – Bristol's floating cider barge.

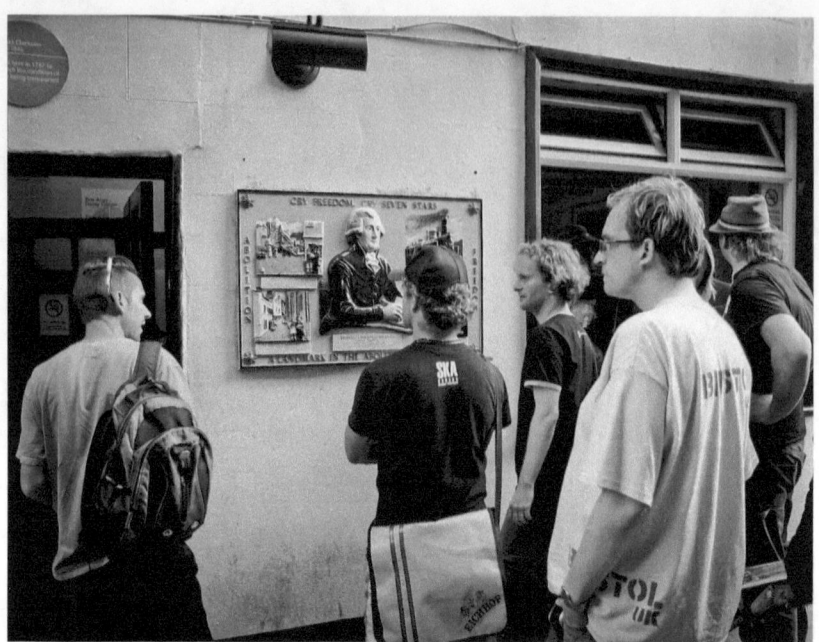

A quick history lesson outside the Seven Stars.

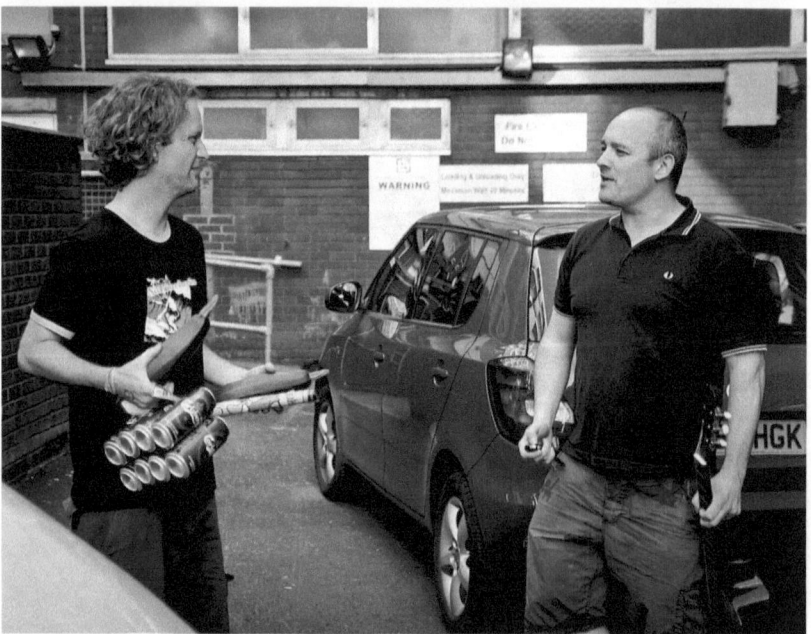

"Hey Jamer... can you play us a tune?"
"Oi Nick... can yer make us a salad?"

This Place Is Awesome

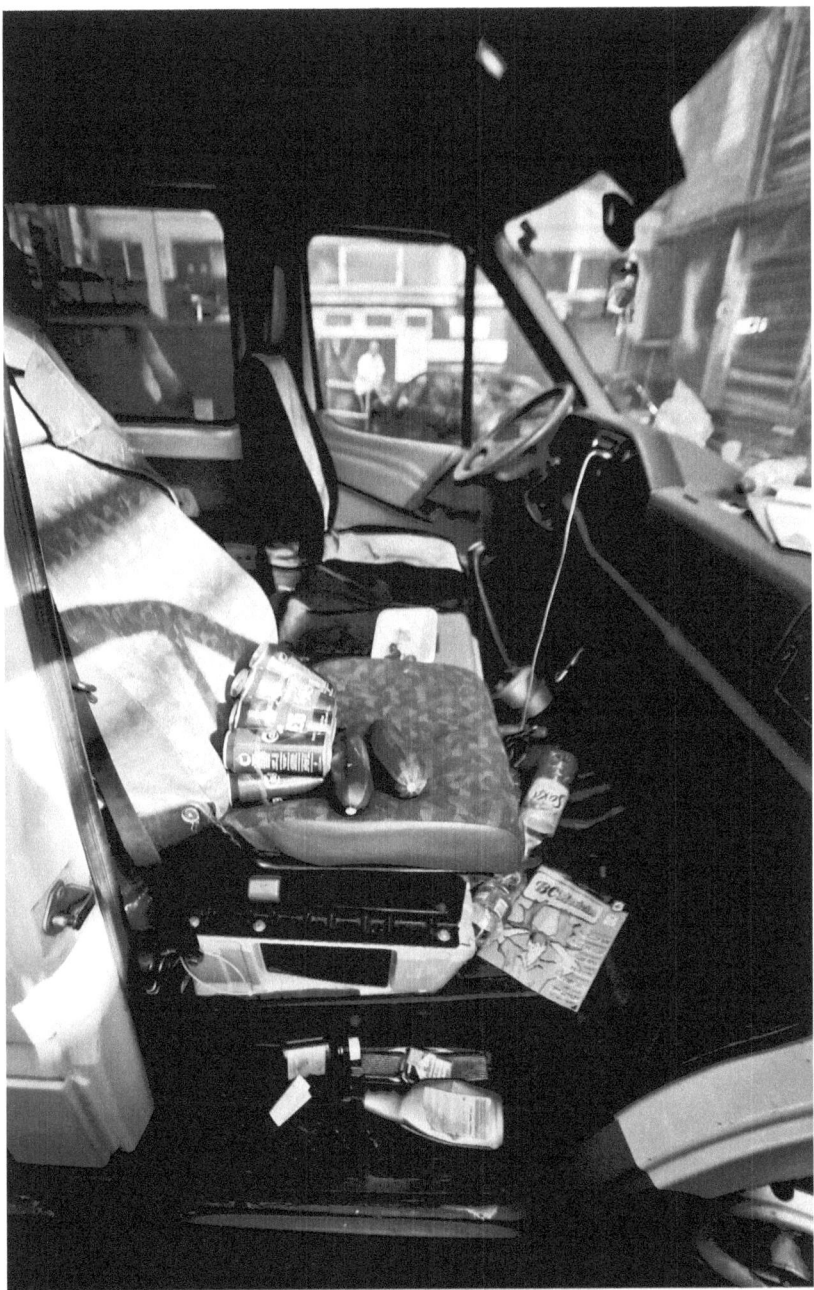

Beer, and zucchinis – standard provisions for the tour van. It seemed like there was always at least one zucchini rolling around the floor of the van at all times. I can't explain why.

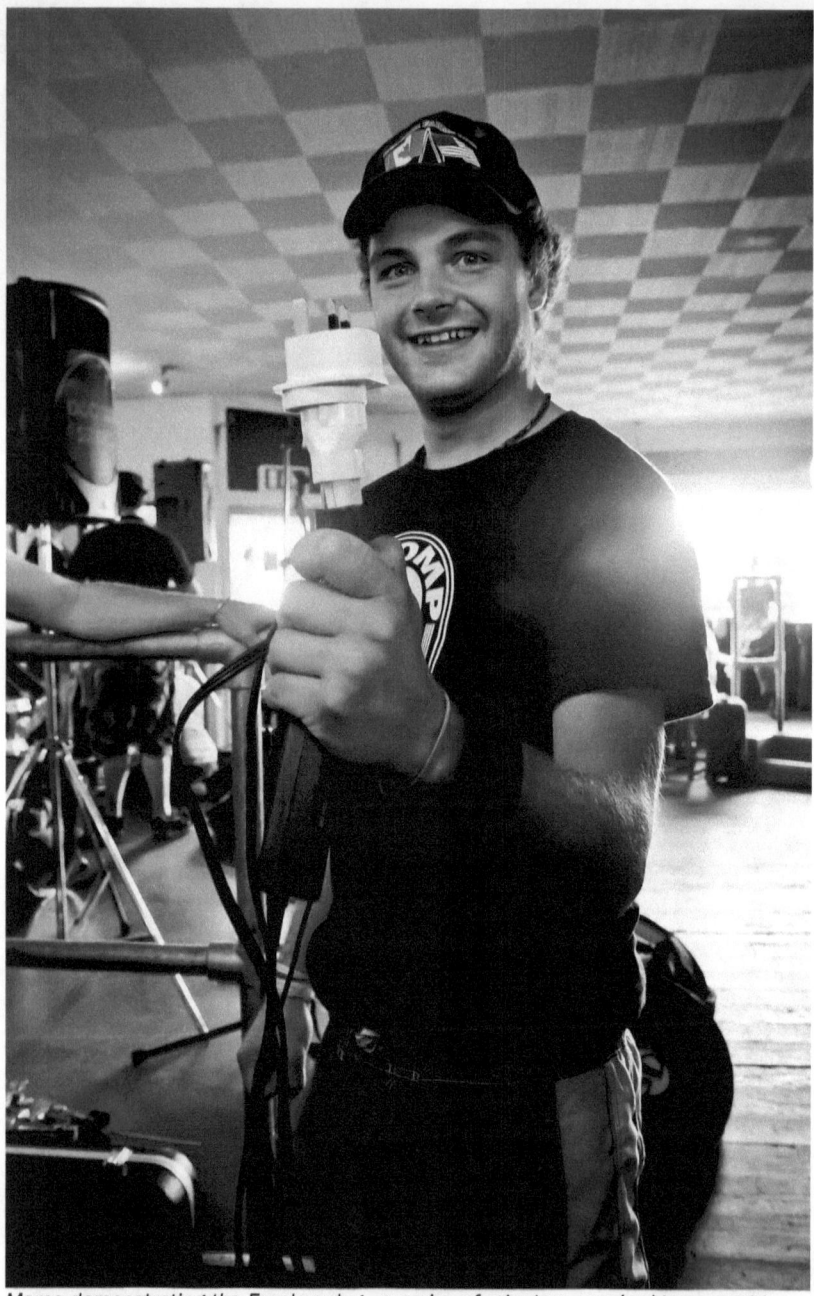

Marco demonstrating the Frankenplug - a series of adapters required to convert to the local "standard." They may have invented democracy, but the Europeans couldn't decide on a single plug design if their very lives depended on it.

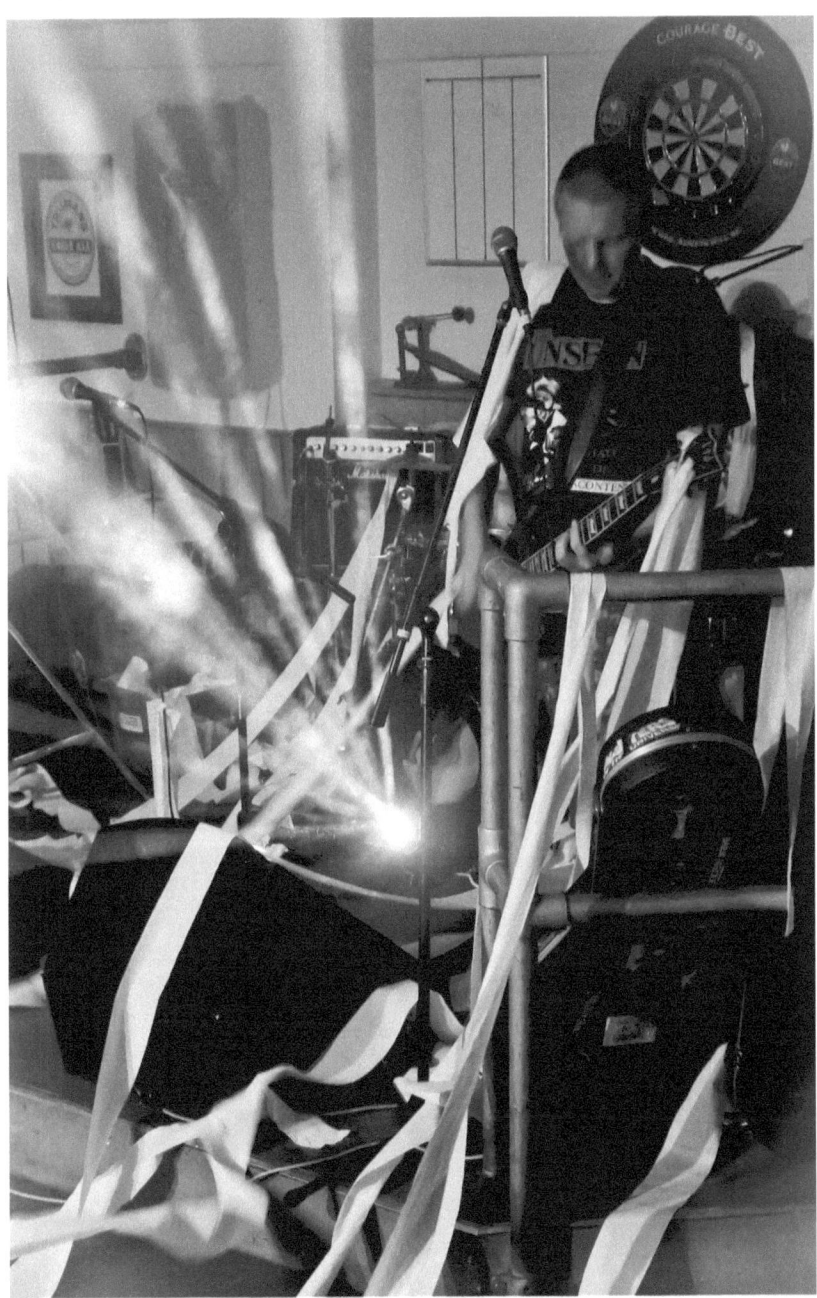

Opening act "Hacksaw" prove that showmanship is not dead by building a stage show out of a single light fixture and many rolls of toilet paper.

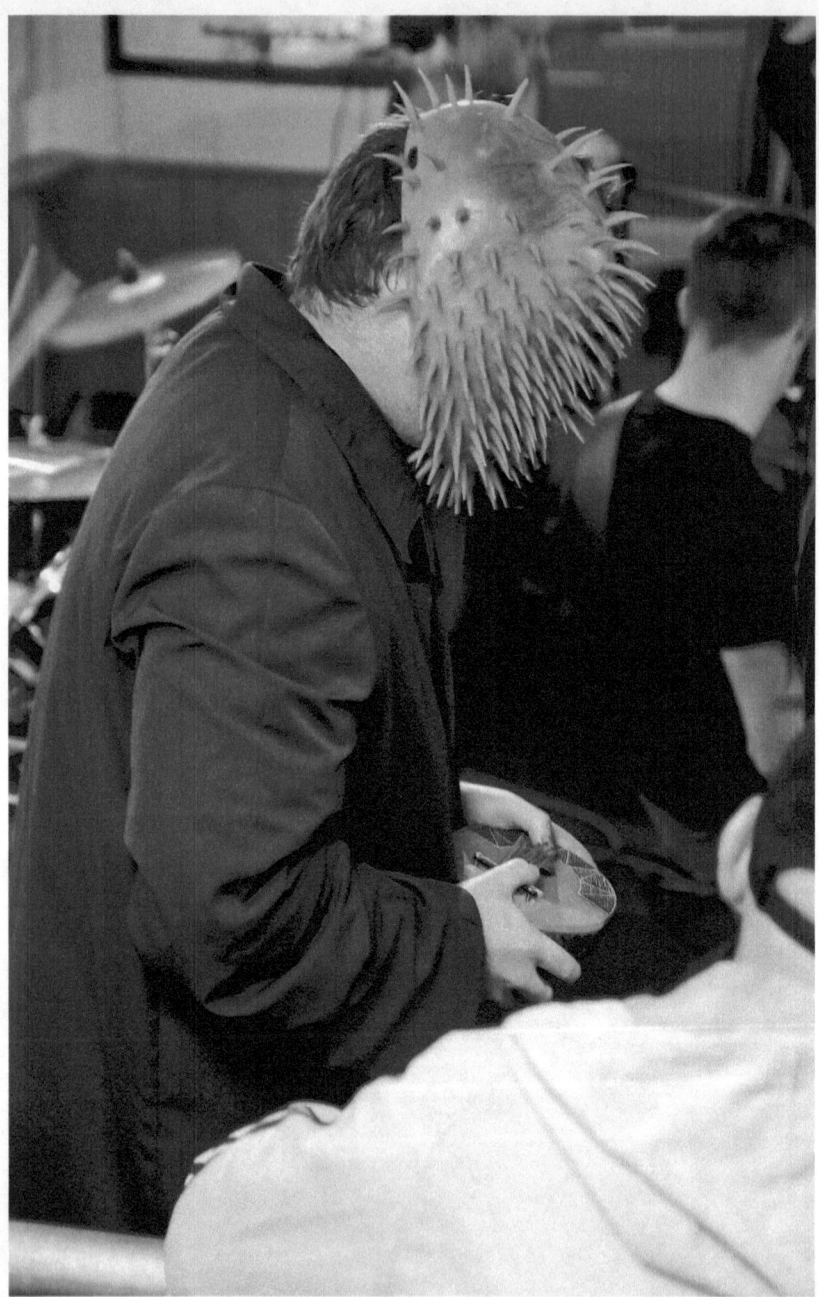
The Surfin Turnips' enigmatic kalimba player.

This Place Is Awesome

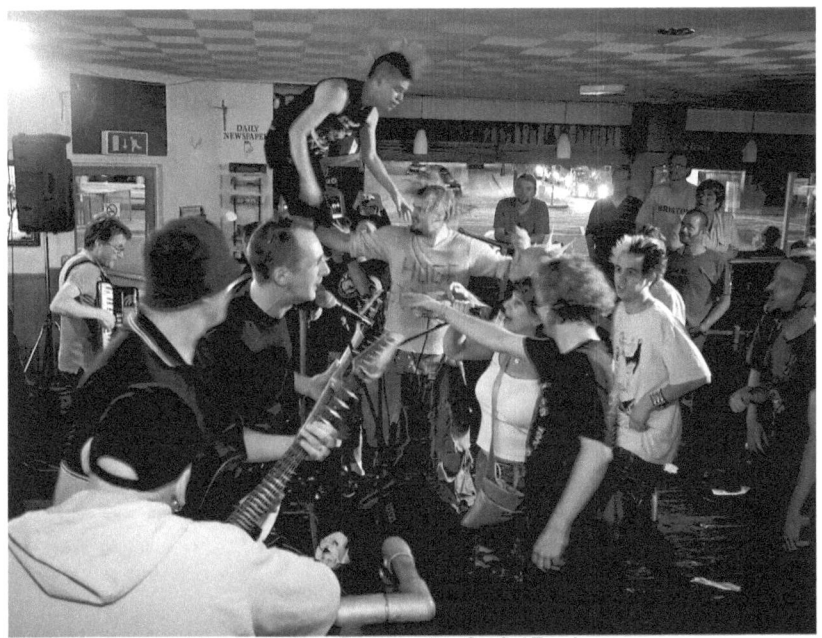

Seamus prepares for a stage dive. Onstage: The Surfin' Turnips.

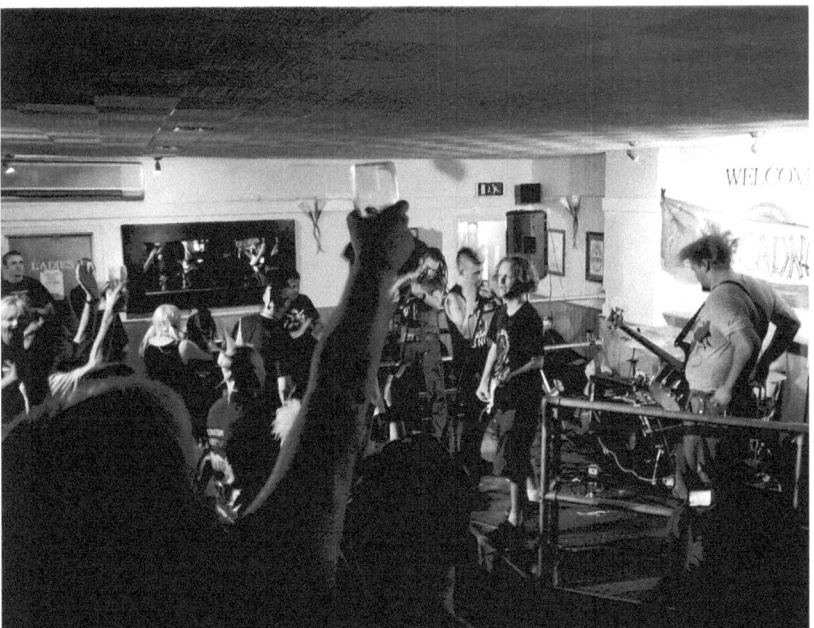

The Dreadnoughts deliver the goods to the audience at The Reckless Engineer.

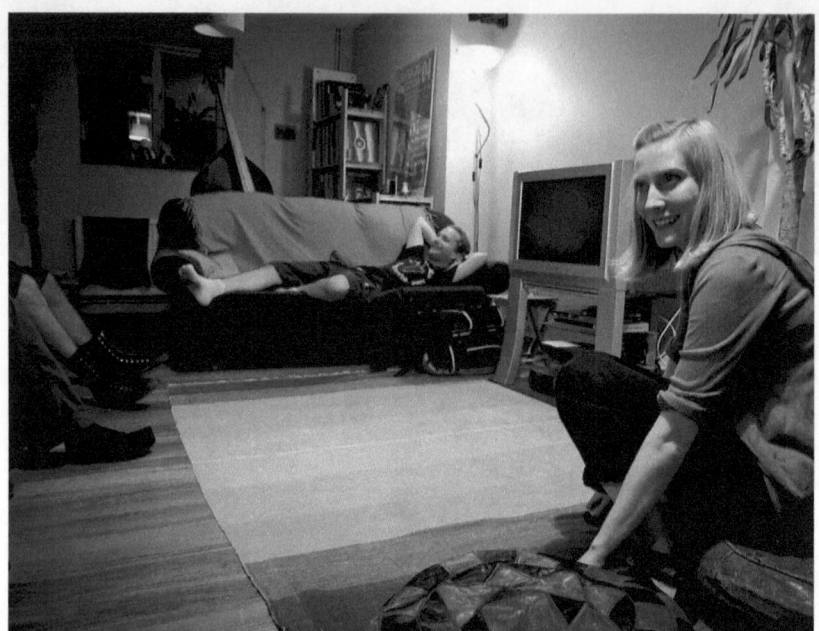

Zoey insists for the 400th time that we "take some comfort," unaware that a couch that wasn't in danger of being carried off by insects in a room that had been cleaned at least once in the last decade was "living in the lap of luxury" for her guests.

THIS IS WHAT I IMAGINED CANADIANS WERE LIKE.

Day Two
July 2 – Bristol, Mudgely, Plymouth

The day started slowly. Nick, Andrew, Drew, and I rose from our bed, couches, and floor respectively and lazily wandered around the house. Seamus and Marco had slept in the van. Once everyone was up and about, the decision was made to walk down to the High Street in search of breakfast. The boys settled easily on a standard English breakfast at a local cafe, which they devoured with inexplicable zeal. I had to wonder just what they'd been eating for the previous month and a half that blood pudding, greasy eggs, and fried tomatoes seemed like something to salivate over. I thought about the time I excitedly told my brother how my new girlfriend had introduced me to the food of her heritage – sushi.

"You need to introduce her to the food of your ancestors now" he said. Our parents are English immigrants to Canada.

"How do I do that?"

"It's easy. Just boil the shit out of anything."

Food is not Britain's greatest gift to the world.

"There are no vegetarians in a tour van" is the modern equivalent of the old line about atheists and foxholes. Seamus gave up his vegetarianism for the most part on this tour. In places like Switzerland and Germany it's virtually impossible not to eat meat. For Seamus, who has no choice about not eating wheat products, the choices start to get very thin. Given the option, Seamus will eat a vegetarian meal, but he had to embrace his inner carnivore more than a few times on this tour.

After breakfast Nick split off from the group to find a doctor who could attend to a vaguely defined, flu-like illness. We left Nick to make his own way down to Plymouth. To this day I am unsure if Nick really was sick, or just sick of being around that same group of people – either seems entirely plausible and understandable to me. He sadly missed what was probably the best day of the British tour, as far as "local colour" was concerned. I sincerely hope he was off quietly and happily experiencing it all in his own way. Lord knows I needed to get away from these clowns after only a few days on the cider express. Sadly, his version of local colour may have been waiting rooms and train stations.

The rest of us spent the morning at St Paul's Carnival, a celebration of Caribbean food, music, and culture that dates back to 1967. Seamus was delighted to find great food in abundance. I basked in the colon-thumping speaker stacks that assaulted me from the sound systems located at every street corner. Andrew caused people to stare and frightened a few small children.

In a moment of curious incongruity, I saw a sticker on a lamppost that said "Resist the 2010 Olympics." Just how pissed off were the people of Bristol about the street closures and overspending on the Olympic Village in Vancouver? It seemed like a hard sell in terms of generating local public outrage.

On returning to Zoey and Kev's place our help was enlisted to bring down some branches that were blocking the satellite dish perched on the top of low roof around the back of the house. Andrew climbed a short ladder and ripped a sapling out of the crag it had rooted in. Zoey was delighted and told us that "this is what I imagined Canadians were like."

"You mean helpful?"

"No, lumberjacks."

I didn't have the heart to tell her that what Andrew had done was more akin to weeding than felling. She seemed so pleased.

Some time around noon, we packed up the van and prepared to head out. En route to Plymouth we were to be escorted by our hosts to the Wilkins Cider Farm, somewhere in the middle of Somerset near a place called Mudgley. Jamer, never one to miss out on a cider-related event, would meet us there.

The drive was calm, pleasant, and largely uneventful in the way that British country roads can be. Any drive across the British countryside on a clear summer day is guaranteed to leave you feeling like you're being filmed for the opening of a new Graham Linehan sitcom. We drove through Cheddar Gorge – the birthplace of the single most popular cheese in the known universe. We passed Glastonbury at a safe distance, although the eponymous festival had been and gone already. I had a feeling we must be getting close when the road turned into a single lane country road. One thing I don't quite understand about the British is why, when the road it twisty and has room for only one vehicle, they insist on planting seven foot high hedges along the sides to give both a sense of claustrophobia and impending doom, as you hurtle along the road unsure if you'll have enough time to stop when a vehicle coming the other direction suddenly appears around a corner. In truth, it's just one of many things I don't understand about the British.

The cider farm was the kind of rustic, warm, cliche of a place, affectionately aged by what was probably centuries of use, that you think only exists in screenwriters' dreams. A collection of old stone and corrugated steel buildings sat on the side of a low hill with a view across the Somerset countryside stretching out to the south. It was all very low key, looking nothing at all like a thriving commercial enterprise. Locals sitting around on doorsteps and brick walls greeted us as we stepped down into an old stone barn and were handed small glass mugs. You can drink as much as you like for free at the farm – you only have to pay for the stuff you take away.

We spent a happy couple of hours wandering the grounds and hanging out in the cool, dark barn. One wall was covered in aging clippings from newspapers and magazine articles about the place. A back room - dusty and filled with cobwebs and old newspapers - was bathed in summer sunshine from the single window and lined with a simple wooden bench where a group of old guys sat drinking and chatting. A rough sign over the door indicated that this was the "lounge."

Scattered around the barn were the tools used to make the cider - large wooden presses, a "scragger" to mash the apples into pulp, local fresh produce for sale, and one of England's most unpleasant snacks, "pork scratchings." Pork scratchings are basically the fat of the pig, deep fried. The texture is a little like corn chips but with two vitally important distinctions. What little taste they possess is, frankly, disgusting, and every bite brings the possible excitement of having to pick a thick, stiff hair out from between your teeth. My dad loves them, but thankfully they seem to be completely unavailable in Canada.

In the main part of the barn three giant wooden casks held "dry," "dry," and "sweet" cider respectively. Mr Wilkins poured our cider into our mugs directly from the wooden spigot, and if asked for "medium" he would simply take half from the dry and half from the sweet.

Roger Wilkins is pretty much what you would expect for a West Country farmer, but without the straw hat. Stocky and white-haired with a weathered face, he is as much a part of the place as the buildings, the air, and the cider. He happily answers questions and shows off the accolades he's been given in a matter of fact tone. The whole place made us feel more like participants than customers.

West Country cider is resolutely different from what most people think of as cider. It's flat, cloudy, and potent. Imagine a lovely, dry apple juice mixed with just a little of the lingering afterburn of ginger beer, then bash yourself unexpectedly in the head with a brick to get the full, final effect. The Wilkins farm is rightly famous for it. Joe Strummer spoke of it as one of his favourite places in the world. John Lydon brought a Dutch film crew around to show them. And The Dreadnoughts drove away from the place with eight gallons of their finest. It would all be gone before the week was out.

This is unpasteurized "zyder," and being the responsible one I asked Roger Wilkins how long it would remain drinkable. "Foiv days avter thee jug az bin open'd." I'm sure he wasn't taking into account the fact that this cider would be kicking around the floor of a warm tour van, where it could pick up all manner of infections and deadly invaders. In hindsight I can imagine a kind of microscopic war of epic proportions, as the yeast and alcohol of the cider valiantly fought against the bacteria and assorted biohazards contained in the unwashed laundry and half-eaten food.

But let me take you back to Bristol again for a moment. I have to get something off my chest.

There have been volumes already written about British plumbing. Lengthy volumes. Lengthy, expletive-filled volumes. And with good cause.

Every culture, it seems has something which is understood and appreciated only by the locals. For the Welsh it's their language (I remember the first time I went there, looking at a map and saying "I can't say that name... there are no fucking vowels in it!"). The Japanese have that weird thing where they number the houses on the street in the order in which they were built. Londoners have their generally inscrutable street system.

And all cultures have their quiet shame. A surprising number of these seem to involve bathrooms. For the British it's their plumbing in general. I woke up in Zoey and Kev's place to a bright, friendly morning. Feeling decently rested I decided to take a shower. Standing naked in the tub, I twiddled knobs (don't go there) and pushed things trying to find hot water – randomly at first and then with an attempt at being methodical when that didn't work. Eventually I decided that I'd just bite the bullet and have a cold shower. People were always taking cold showers in the 1970s sitcoms I grew up with, and it never seemed to bring them to harm. I guess there's a reason why you never actually *saw* them take a cold shower and it has nothing to do with nudity. It's not a nice thing to watch. For me it involved lots of jerking limbs away from the icy water and screaming. I swore I'd never do that again. I very nearly kept that promise.

OK, back on the road. Marco, the designated and sole driver of the van, had to get out of the Wilkins' driveway. He had to turn the van (a standard shift beast with all the helpful attitude of a customs agent) around without hitting an array of stone walls, ditches, and other cars. It was like a videogame. Everyone cheered when he managed it – even the locals... and especially the owners.

We headed for Plymouth, but without the benefit of the GPS, which had disappeared amongst the flotsam, jetsam, and just plain filthsam of the van. Trying to find something small in that moving disaster area was like trying to find a fart in a Jacuzzi. Nevertheless we made it to Plymouth without too much fuss and picked up Nick at the railway station. Nick seemed unchanged, but then I wasn't particularly aware of how this mystery illness was manifesting to begin with. Many months later I was informed that he was, indeed, ill with some kind of common virus. Nick's ability to keep his physical condition under tight wraps was evidently just the same as his notorious ability to keep his emotional state well camouflaged. To be fair, the entire band has been self-described as "avoidant." Nick is just the most notably so, given his status as the expected "leader" of the group.

With the band all safely back together we headed for the venue.

The gig was at a trendy pub that had constructed a tent over the patio in front and evidently put on shows there, much to the delight of the whole neighbourhood I would imagine. The band hid in a spacious upstairs green room that was outfitted with plentiful food and places to sit until it was their turn to go on stage. The crowd was not a typical Dreadnoughts audience. Instead of mohawks, Doc Martens, and body odour, this crowd was more a high heels and Axe body spray kind of affair. The Brits have a notoriously precarious relationship with alcohol. It seems to bring out their best clothes and their worst behaviour. The crowd this night was rowdy, with more than a couple of fights breaking out. Which is kind of ironic, because back on their home turf the audiences dress to look much more aggressive and tough, but I'm not sure I've ever seen a single fight. They'll demolish a mic stand like it had just felt up their sister, but they are civilised towards each other. This Plymouth crowd, who looked more like affluent university students, left the stage alone and had a go at each other instead.

When the band played their cover of the Surfin' Turnips' "Cider," Seamus put down his fiddle and took over the vocals. He climbed onto Andrew's shoulders, making a bass player/singer chimera that stood a good ten or eleven feet tall and had become known as the "Tower of Power." Andrew kept playing while Seamus flailed around with a mic in one hand and, in this case, a gallon jug of Wilkins cider in the other. The whole thing could clearly collapse at any moment, evoking images of a miniaturised version of what would happen if the Eiffel Tower decided to take a nap on top of Paris.

The soundboard had long been forgotten behind a wall of people at this point, so it was a bit unnerving to hear a disembodied voice booming out of the monitors.

"OK boys, let's settle down a little."

I'm unclear on whether the band won the audience over, or if they would have showed enthusiasm for anyone who was prepared to be as rowdy as they were. What I can say is that there is an inescapable, unpretentious, infectious charm to these five dingy characters. The band's preferences lean towards the black leather and mohawk crowd, and they will go as far as to be verbally dismissive of many other constituencies, but when they break into their act it's hard for anyone not to get swept up.

After the show it came time to figure out where to sleep. For the whole week I was with them, and for the whole three month tour I have to assume, they seemed to take a pathological approach to avoiding things that would make their lives easier. The rider stipulated a meal, so dinners were always assured and frequently decent. But they were in charge of finding their own accommodations. Now call me crazy, but on arriving in a strange town and knowing that I'd be exhausted in a few hours, perhaps the first statement out of my mouth to a local ear would have been "please spread the word that we need a place to stay tonight." And yet it seemed to be the most "after" of afterthoughts. Frequently one, many, or even sometimes all of the band members would end up sleeping in the van. The van could sleep one person in acceptable comfort or two to three people uncomfortably. If the other two were also forced to sleep there they would be dreaming of Abu Graib. Perhaps they were embarrassed at the level of economy they were being forced to adopt. Maybe it was some kind of ongoing dare. I wouldn't rule out simple, profound laziness. Or perhaps it was just another example of the peculiar lack of organisation that infected elements of the tour.

Here's another example. Not one of them was traveling with a cell phone.

Think about that for a moment. Not only does that mean that there's no simple way for them to contact their booking agent or the next venue, and no way for the next venue to contact them if there's a problem, but it also means that none of them can ever go off on their own for a while because it would be impossible to find them if they were needed. They were always together because no one could ever leave. Email filled in a lot of the less immediate communications needs, but imagine not being able to contact the person you're traveling with to say "we need to leave in half an hour." Me, I'd have become a solo act within the first week and hoped that no one discovered the bodies.

And yet I never saw them arrive late for a show. They were always at sound check on time, they took the stage at the right time, and the shows were complete, if consistently rowdy and occasionally a bit ramshackle. So they had the necessary organisation to pull that off.

So it was that we were left, in the early morning hours, without a plan for accommodations in Plymouth. The others suggested that Nick was "ready to crack," so it was decided that he and I would share a hotel room and he could have a break. Nick and I would split a hotel room one more time on this tour, but that time it would be me that was showing signs of stress fractures around the base of the psyche.

Nick and I wandered, exhausted, through the dark, empty streets of Plymouth, heading in the general direction of the waterfront where we knew there to be hotels. We were looking for a giant illuminated "Holiday Inn." It's the upside of globalism – consistency and familiarity when you need it most.

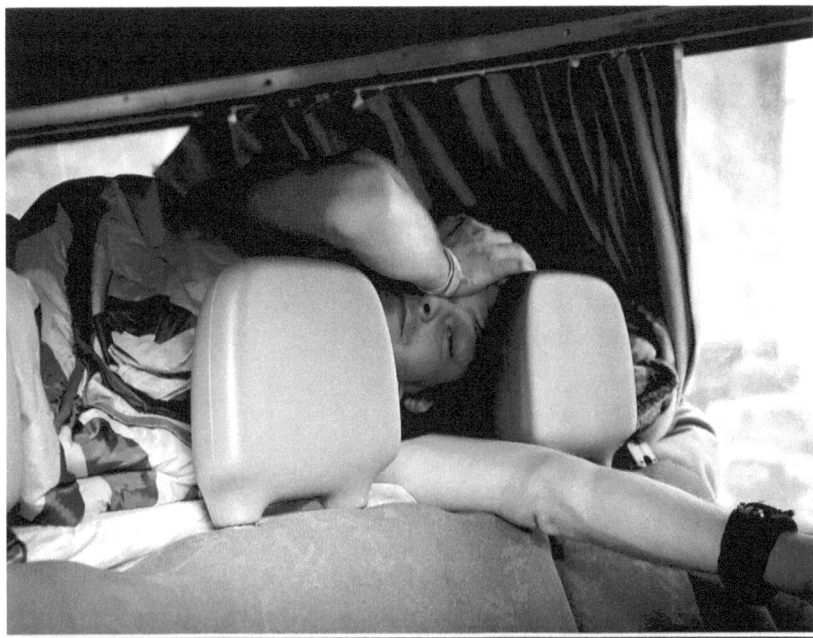

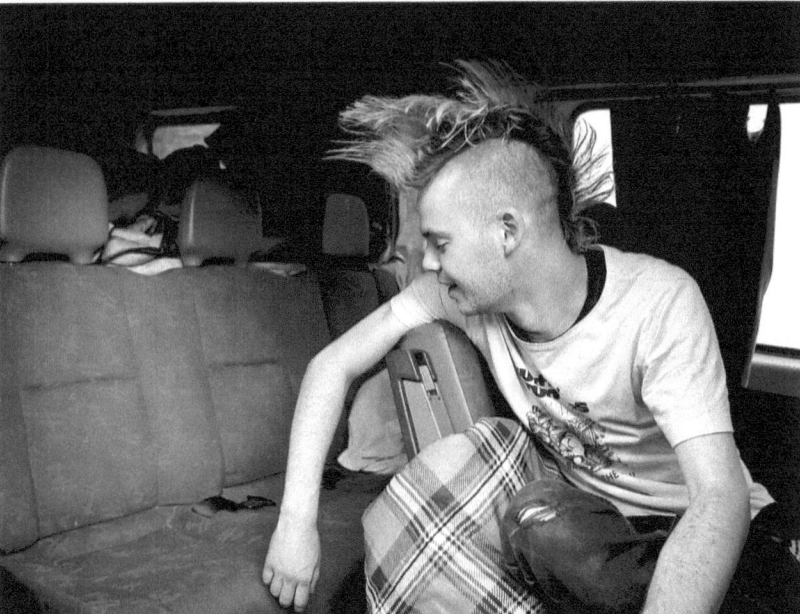

Marco and Seamus begin the long, slow process of recovering from a night sleeping in the van. Being hungover the next morning didn't help when you're waking up in a van, but being drunk the night before was an essential part of falling asleep in one.

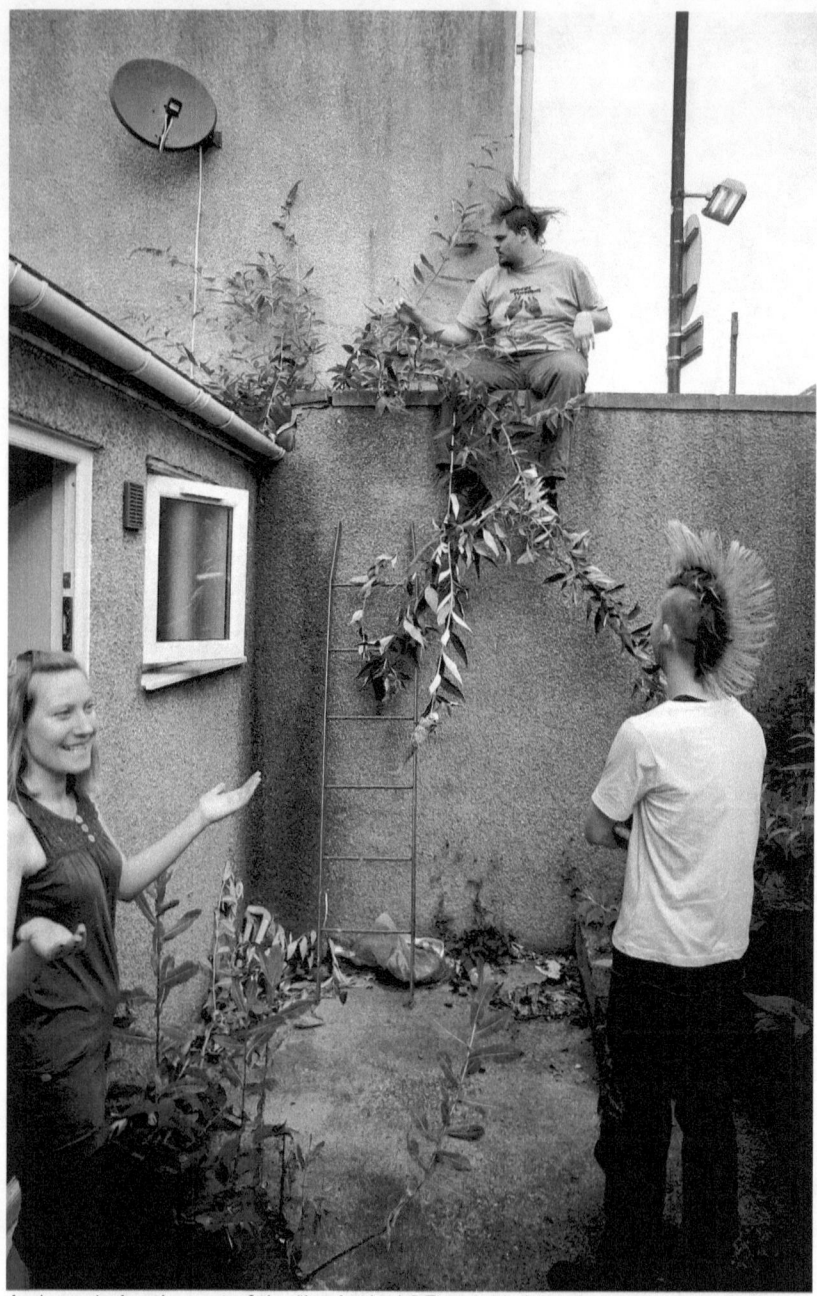

Andrew playing the part of the "lumberjack." Zoey is delighted to have a real Canadian to help deal with the forest growing on the roof of their shed.

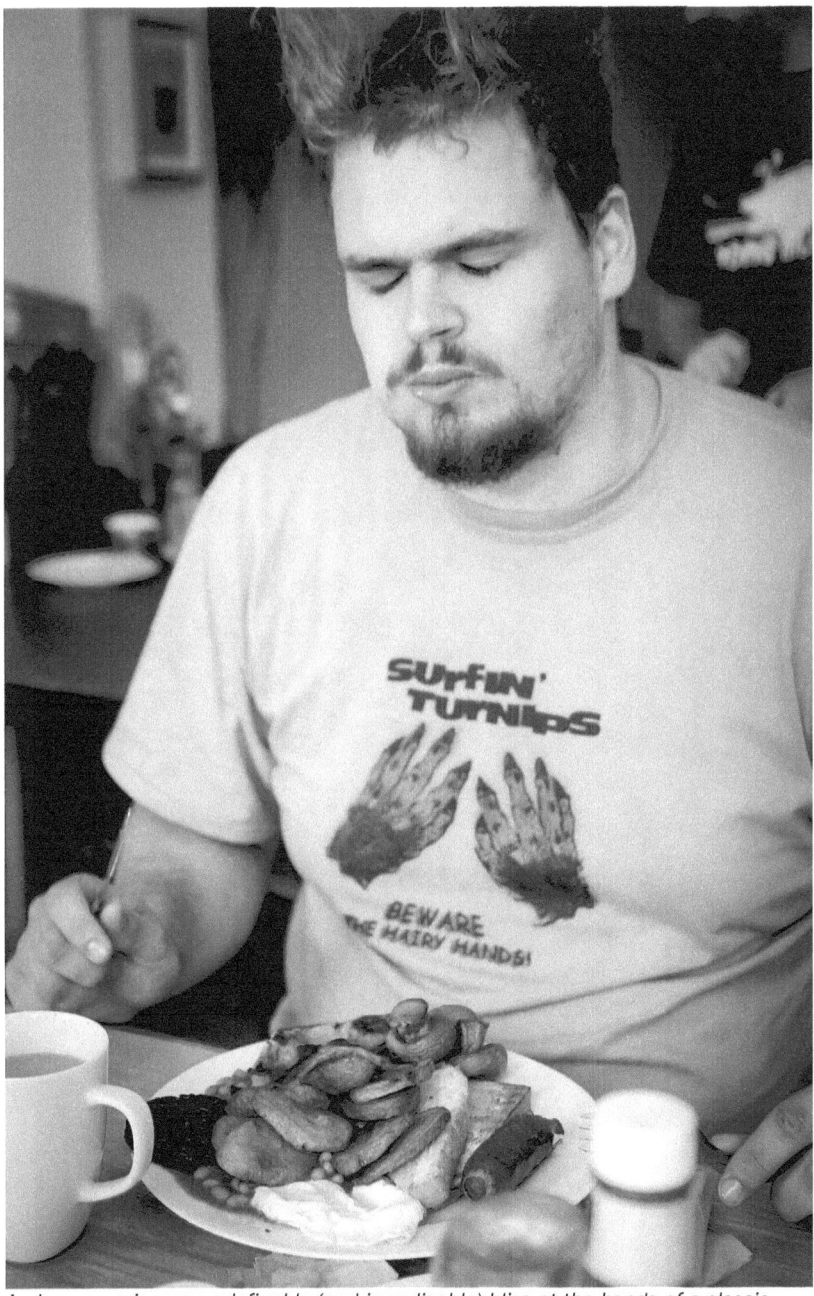

Andrew experiences undefinable (and inexplicable) bliss at the hands of a classic English breakfast.

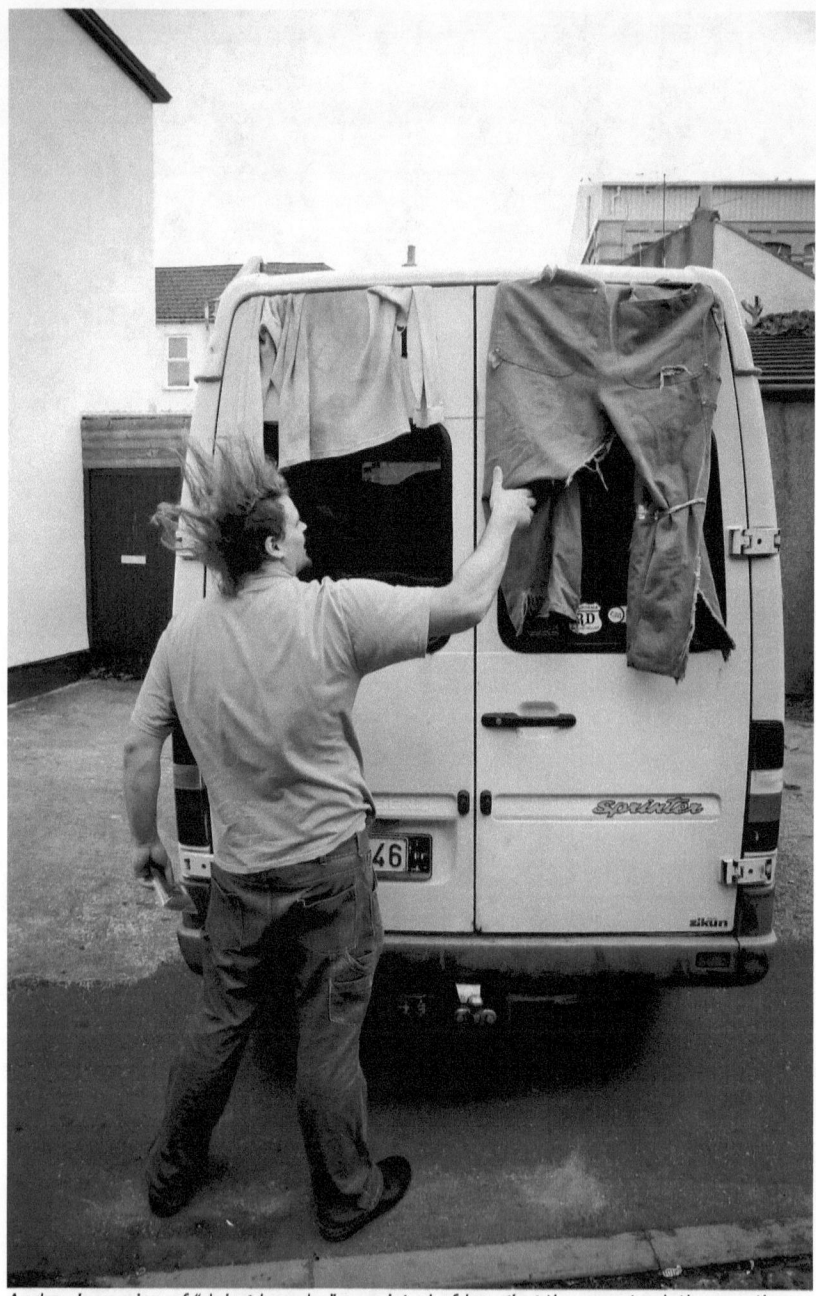

Andrew's version of "doing laundry" consisted of hanging the sweaty clothes on the back of the van after the show and taking them down the next morning. Oddly enough, no one ever stole either the pants or the "gig shirt."

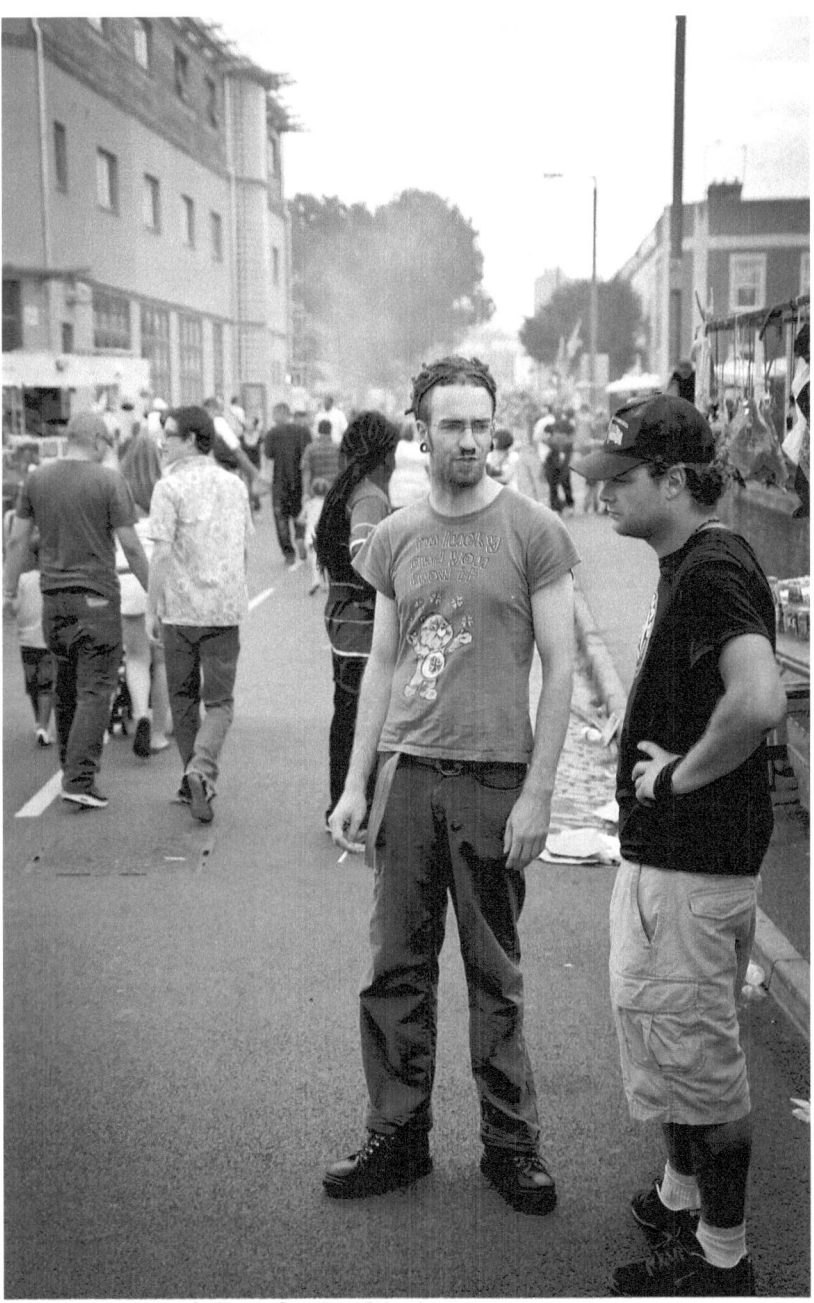

Drew and Marco at St Paul's Carnival, Bristol.

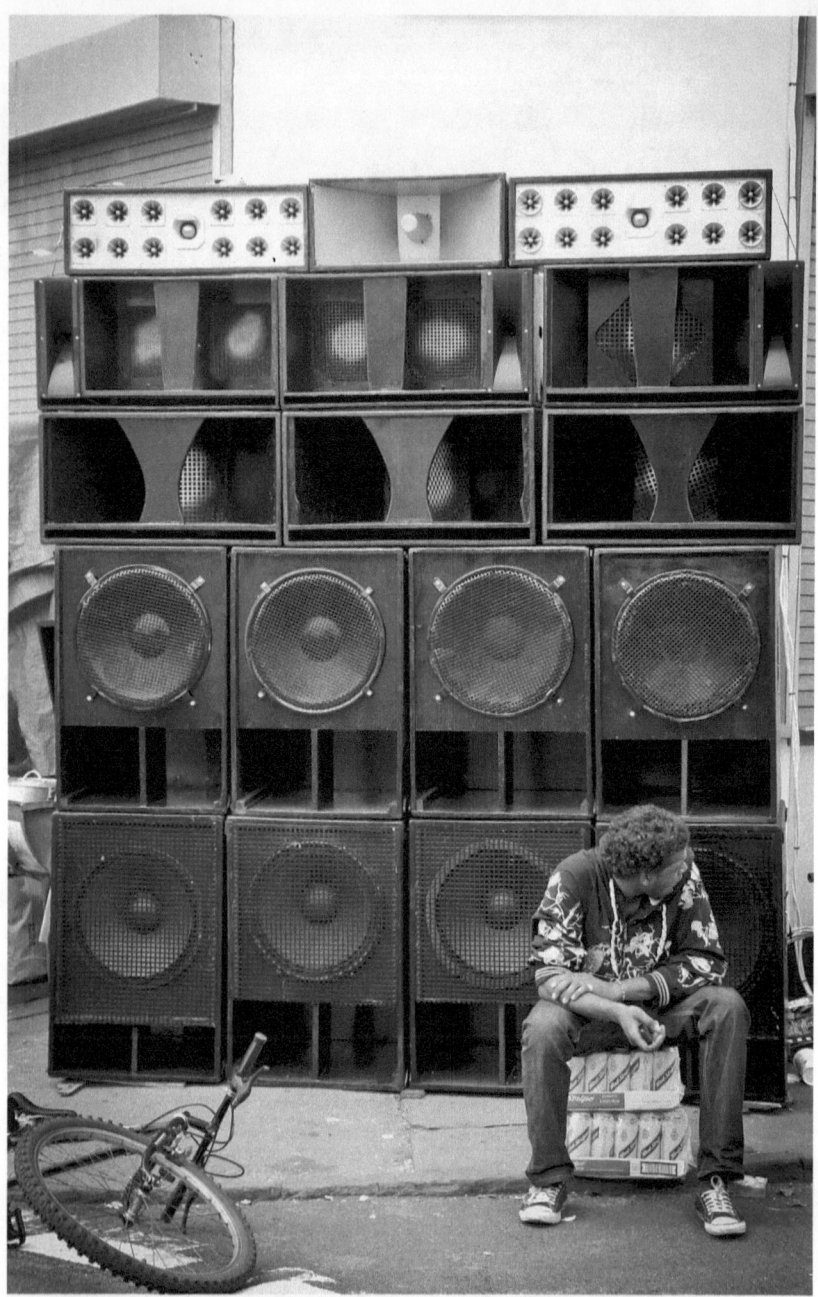

A Carnival sound system. One of many. I'm not sure what force of nature
or brand of super glue was able to keep this man from being bounced across
the street by the sound.

This Place Is Awesome

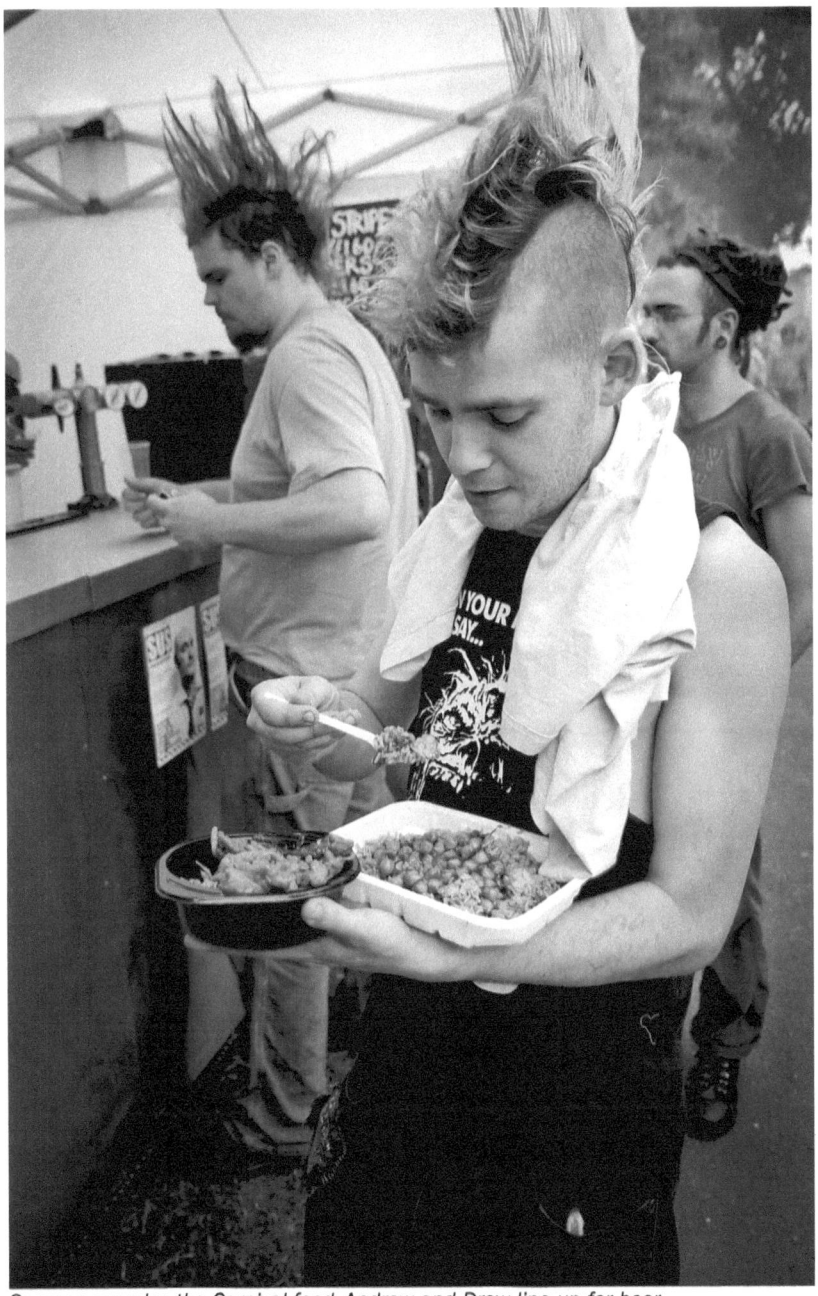

Seamus samples the Carnival food. Andrew and Drew line up for beer.

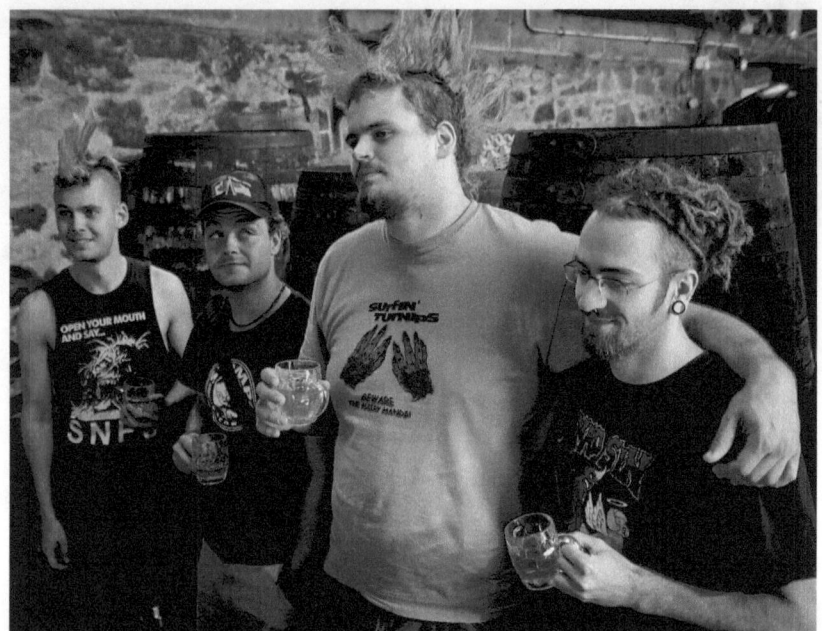

The boys (minus Nick) at the Wilkins Cider Farm. The barrels behind them contain "dry" and "sweet" varieties. If you want "medium" they pour half from one and half from the other.

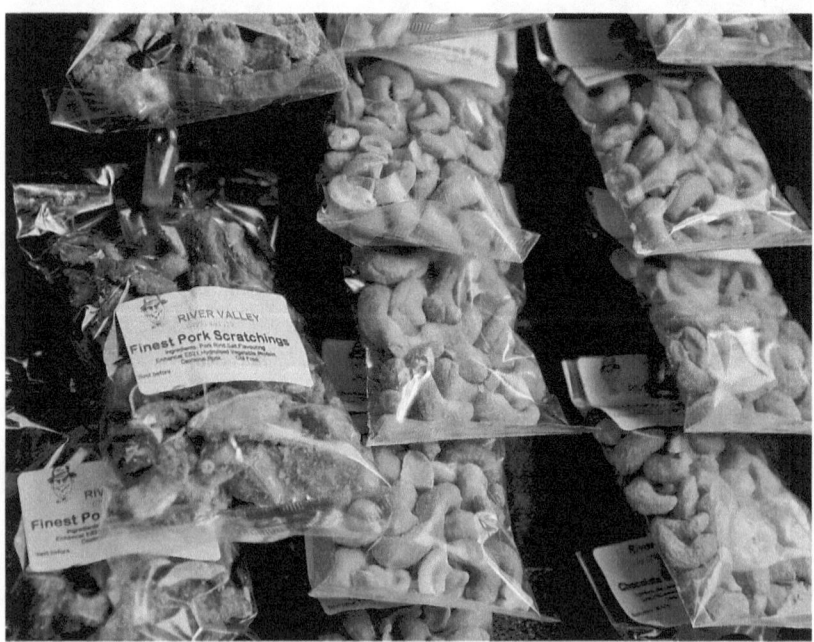

"Finest Pork Scratchings." Words simply fail me.

This Place Is Awesome

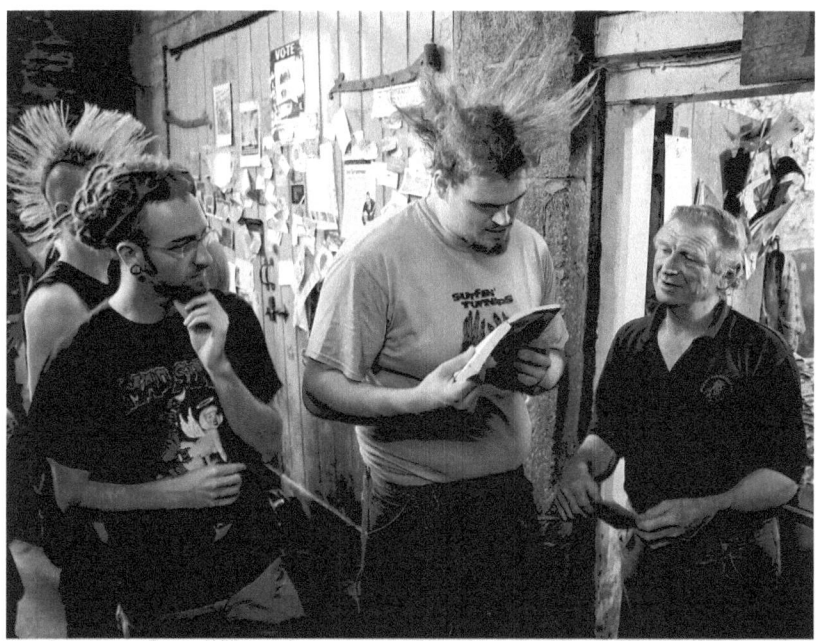

The legendary Roger Wilkins shares some of the history of the farm with the Drews.

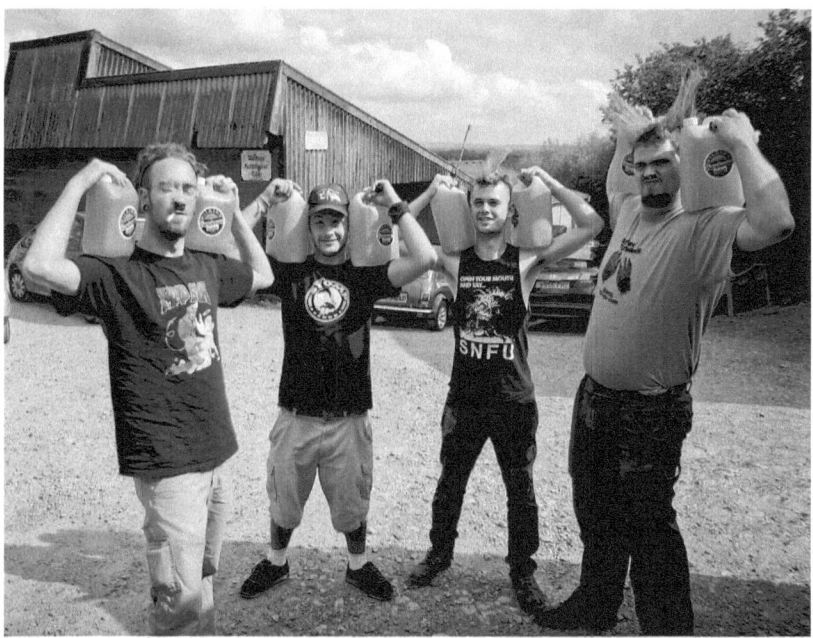

Eight gallons of liquid gold.

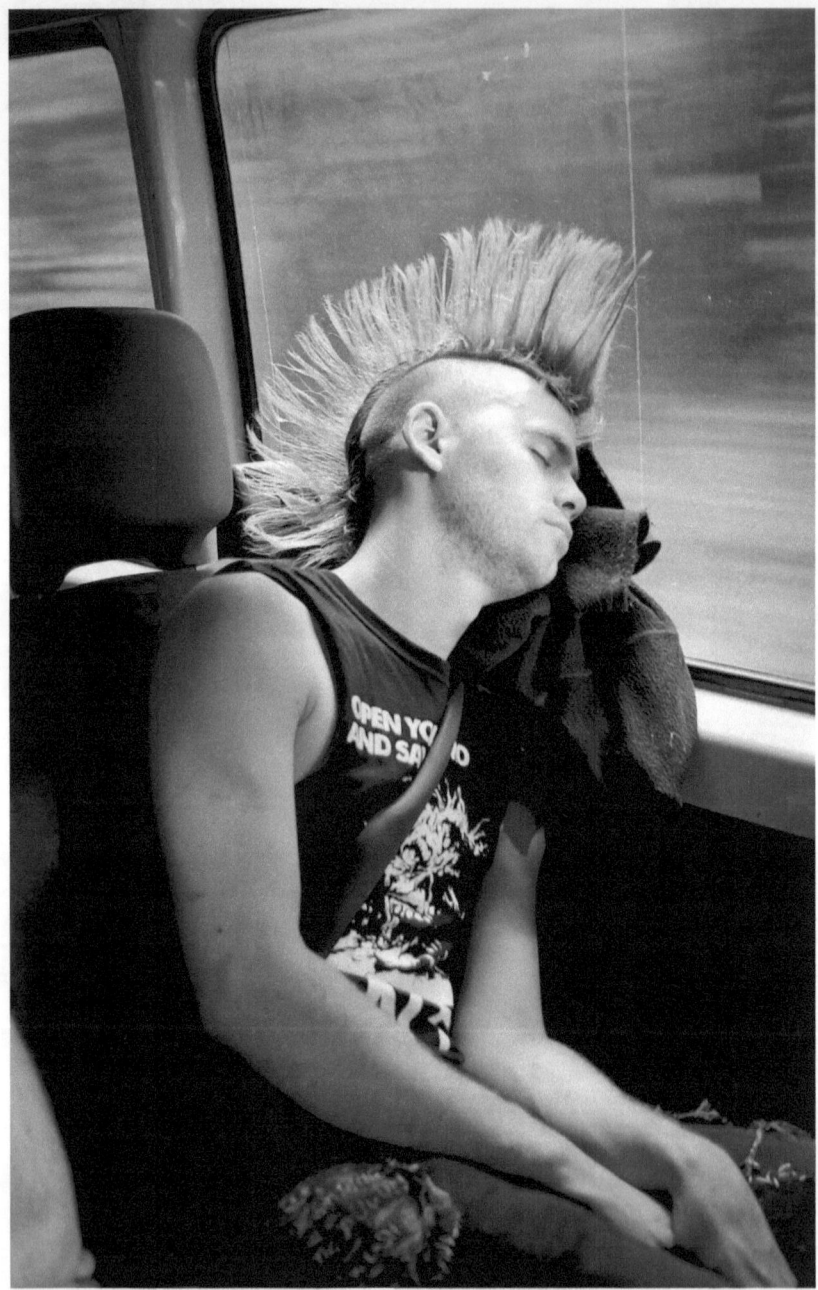

Sleeping is on a "catch as catch can" basis. Seamus passes out on the drive to Plymouth.

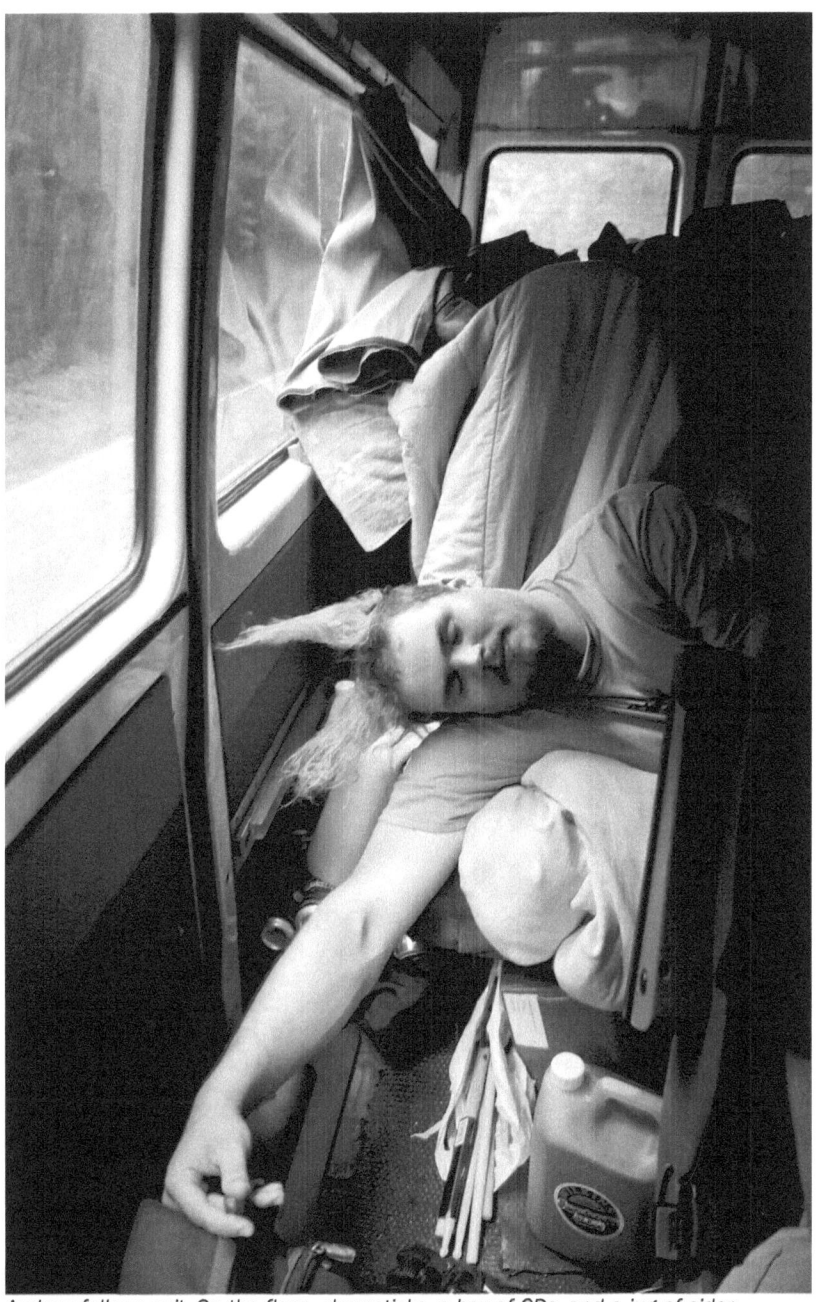

Andrew follows suit. On the floor - drumsticks, a box of CDs, and a jug of cider.

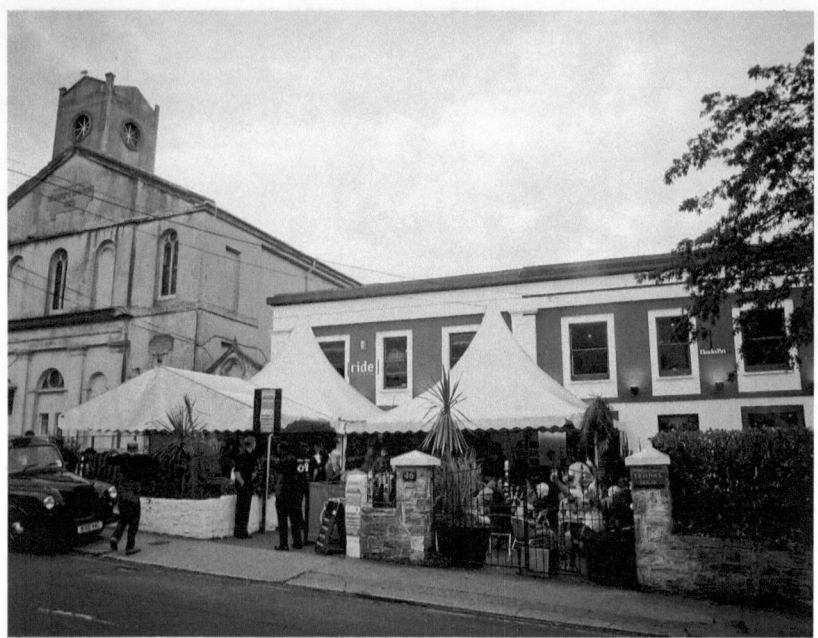

The Plymouth venue - the "ride." The band played under the tent out front.

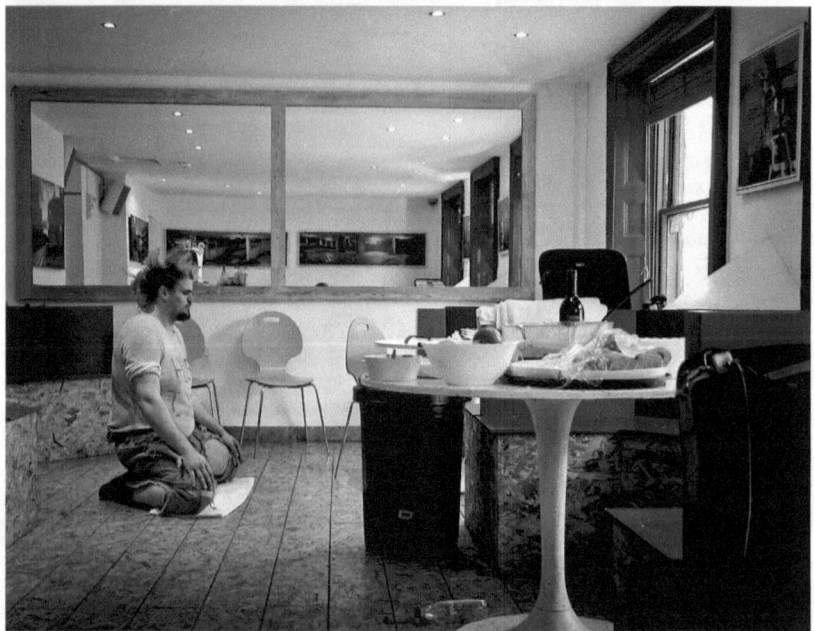

Scenes from the green room. Andrew, a keen student of Aikido, takes a moment to sort himself out before the show.

This Place Is Awesome

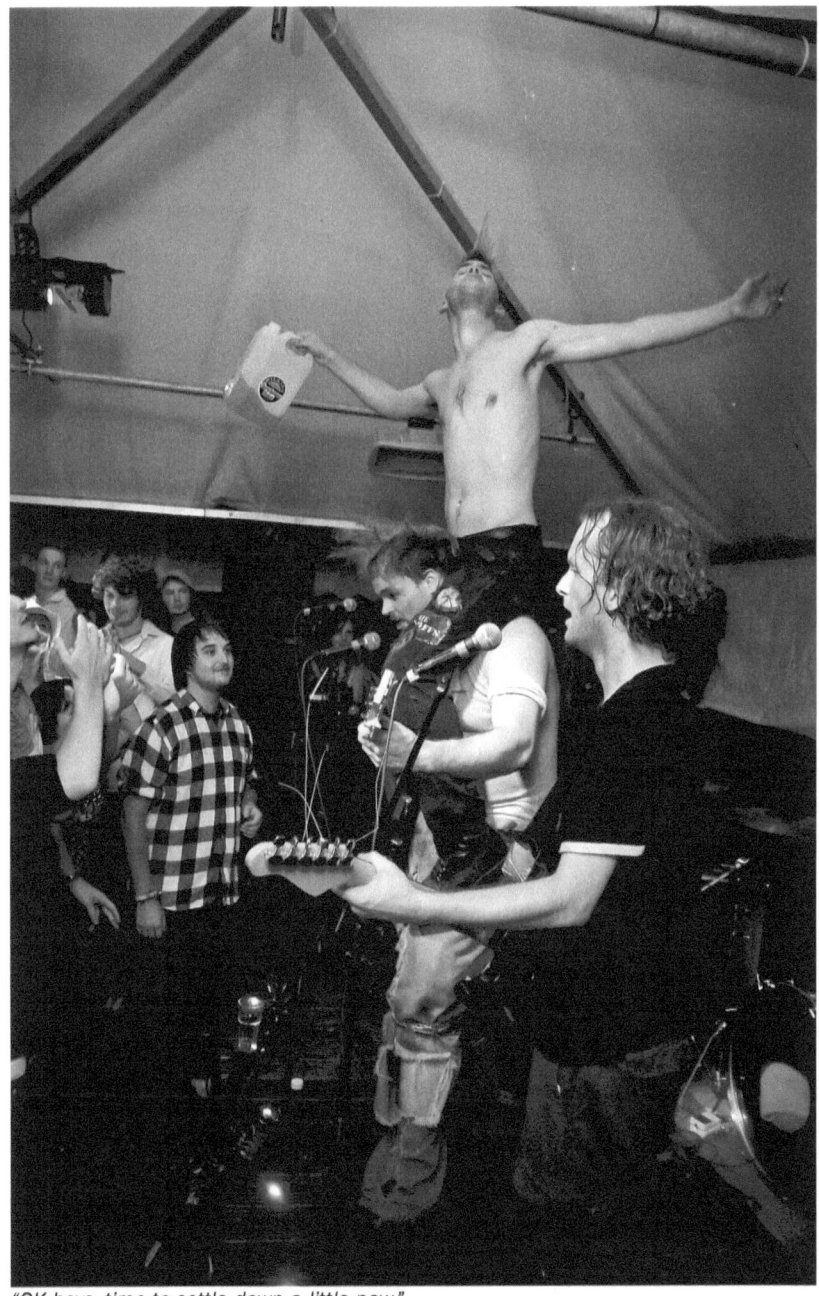

"OK boys, time to settle down a little now."

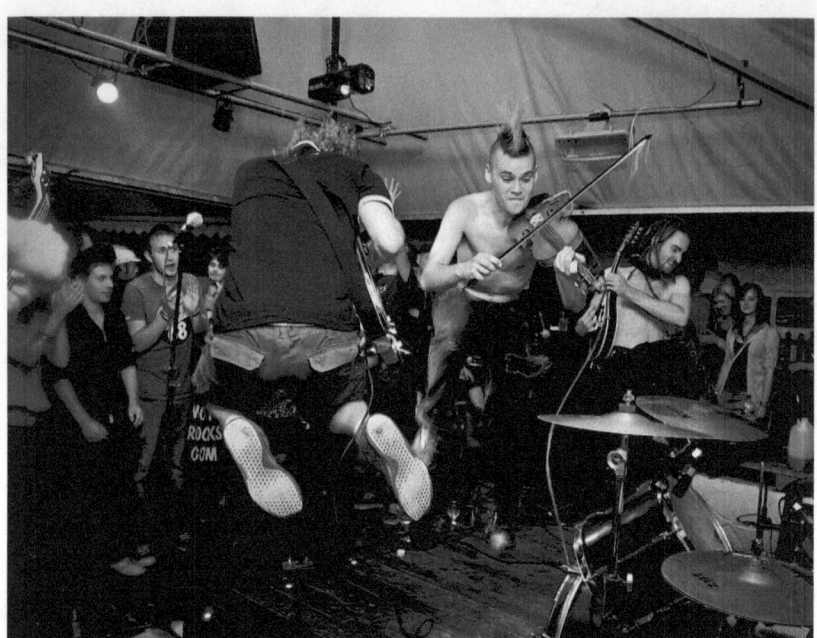

"Houston, we have liftoff."

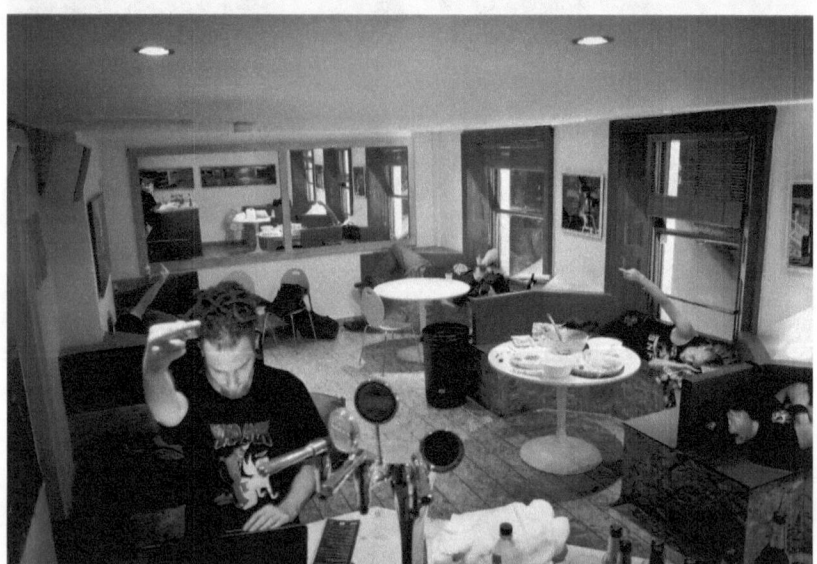

There is room for everyone to flake out for a moment and show the photographer how much they respect him, post show.

This Place Is Awesome

LOOK AT THIS PLACE, IT'S AWESOME.

Day Three
July 3 – Plymouth, Chepstow

I woke up in a real bed with real sheets and it was quiet. Nick had his head covered with a pillow, as it had been for most of the night. He'd had enough of Andrew's snoring, which is prodigious, so I think it became instinct for him to cover his head while he slept. Seamus snored when he'd been drinking, which is to say every night. Drew didn't sleep well, so he tossed and turned all night. Nick probably hadn't had a decent night's sleep in weeks. But being the type that would rather suffer than confront an issue, he just sucked it up and trickled out the exhaustion and frustration a little at a time. The others called him a "ticking time bomb at this point" but the truth was that they were probably all not far from cracking.

Marco and Seamus are the most adept at surviving this sort of thing. They have the most laissez faire attitude and are willing to put up with all manner of abuse. Marco is the most likely to do it with a smile. He's a peculiar character. A happy go lucky type with stunningly low standards for many things, he's also highly driven and extremely hard working at times. He is the most organised in many ways, which is a sad commentary but it's also true that the tour would not have happened without him. His unstoppable cheeriness is a marvel. Maybe he's insane.

Nick and I packed up and walked back to the venue to find Seamus sitting on the low stone wall in front. The rest of the band had survived the night in the van and were determined to find the missing GPS. It was found after the entire van got emptied out onto the street. For some reason this inventory-taking exercise triggered something in what was left of their minds and they realised how filthy the van was. Maybe they were embarrassed that an outsider was seeing, in detail, what they had been reduced to.

Out of nowhere emerged three unusual sights. The first was an air freshener, which broke after one day – I have a theory it was the first ever case of an inanimate object committing suicide. Shortly after that a truck stop portable vacuum appeared and made a desperate attempt at cleaning up in spite of the fact that it had all the sucking power of an asthmatic bushtit. Most amusing of all was the sight of Nick sprinkling baking soda over all the surfaces, like he was trying to remove the faint whiff of garlic from the fridge. (I had to question the wisdom of sprinkling white powder all over the floor of a van full of musicians that would shortly be attempting to drive across the border.)

While the boys were reloading the van, the clouds opened and a three minute torrential downpour followed. Marco noted "I love how when it started raining your first instinct was to take pictures." Many would have said that with resentment and annoyance. He genuinely thought it was funny.

The van was everything you might expect, and less. It was a Mercedes passenger/freight van – about the length of a typical Canadian van but with an exceptionally high ceiling. They go under the name "Sprinter" here. The back had a plywood platform that stored gear underneath and served as a bed on top. The back seat was missing the middle seatbelt, forcing me to tie the two far ends together in a reef knot, in a desperate attempt to avoid flying through the windshield or getting a ticket. The windshield wipers didn't work and the doors didn't close properly. To get the rear door to stay latched required a carefully aimed backhand punch that evoked memories of The Fonz. Only two of the windows were functional and the gear shift bore an unnatural and uncomfortable resemblance to a part of a male horse's anatomy that is usually only seen in the presence of female horses. Seriously. It was a bit weird that way.

And of course the outside suffered more battle scars as time went on. In Britain alone we left half the paint from the right side on a post behind the venue in Bristol, part of the rear bumper on someone's garden wall in

Stoke, and I'm proud to say that I contributed a large scrape across the roof, courtesy of a low ceiling in Newcastle. Early on in the tour I asked about the source of the van. Marco gleefully pulled out a handwritten rental agreement that looked like a forged high school absent note and explained how they rented it from some odd sounding guy in Belgium. "He does this all the time" I was told. "That doesn't fill me with confidence" I replied.

I asked about insurance and almost instantly thought better of it. But it was insured. Well, more accurately "it insured."

Evidently the band, in a fit of foresight and responsibility that was probably the last one of the tour, rang up the owner of the van as they were driving away and asked about insurance.

"It insured" was the response.

"But what is it insured for? Theft? Collision?"

"Oh, it insured" (this time with greater confidence)

"How much is it insured for? What do we do if there's an accident?"

"It insured."

It was clear they weren't going to get any further, so they left it at that. Every time there was a mishap, or the possibility of one, the van would erupt in five voices cheerfully yelling "it insured! it insured!"

There were never any arguments over what music was played over the van's stereo. They were able to plug their iPods in and a broad range of styles came out. NOFX was a regular favourite, and on one occasion led to an unlikely and doomed attempt by Seamus to crowd surf inside the van. With only two sets of hands to try to support him it ended in a heap somewhere in the middle of the backseat, amidst peels of howling laughter

As we drove from Plymouth to Chepstow the soundtrack eventually turned to a gypsy band from Finland with a name no one could pronounce. The Dreadnoughts were soaking up the musical influences on this trip, storing them away for the future.

Unfortunately the sound from the stereo was utter crap. There was no bass speaker. They would complain about how every time the stereo started up, the bass reverted back to its default level which was too high for the tiny dashboard speaker. What no one seemed to notice was that the system appeared to be stuck in shop demonstration mode. Breathlessly excited messages about its many amazing features and functions would scroll across the LCD display, and every time it started up it would reset itself back to the beginning.

En route to Chepstow, Nick stuck his hand out the window at 150kmph in the rain. He commented on how the drops hurt like hell at that speed. Nick and Marco discussed terminal velocity. Marco said that a mouse can fall out of an airplane and survive. Nick figured that that wasn't fair.

Meanwhile Drew tried to make a holder for the GPS out of duct tape, so that it could be taped to the dash then removed easily. It had been giving them wrong directions all morning, so they unplugged it. I was able to fill in using my iPhone, which even with poor internet reception safely guided us to Wales.

The GPS, these occasional failures not withstanding, was clearly a brilliant investment. A country like England, with it's inscrutably winding, convoluted street arrangements, is a unique kind of nightmare to navigate, even for the locals. London cabbies are required to pass a test to prove they have what is termed "the knowledge." They might dedicate three years of their lives to the intense learning and driving practice in the city required to prepare for the test. MRIs have shown that internalising the insanely complex street maps has a physical affect on their brains. You are tempting fate to enter any good-sized British city without an aid. For years these took the form of the "A to Z Guides" – street indexes that needed to be at a high resolution to be able to show the necessary detail of streets that can be shorter than an American's driveway. These days it's more economical, both in monetary cost and the amount of storage space required, to have a GPS.

The Dreadnoughts named their GPS "Julia." It has to do with Neil Hamburger.

Neil Hamburger, for the uninitiated, is an American performer. He is evidently considered a comic. His material consists of one-liners and short quips, delivered deadpan style, and mostly deriving their humour from being outrageous. Not outrageously clever, or outrageously funny, or outrageously strange, just outrageous in that "I can't believe he just said that" kind of way. And it formed a staple of the soundtrack for the tour van.

I'll make no bones about it – I find him tedious, dull, and pointless. The boys figured this out quickly and tried very hard to torment me by playing it repeatedly, and delivering the jokes themselves at regular intervals.

At one point Nick, Seamus, and I attempted to discuss the artistic merit of Neil Hamburger. The debate went on in exactly the way one might predict. It's like trying to put a value on art; it's a slippery argument that refuses to accept anything definitive from either side. I needed to try to put a cap on it so I explained that it is expected that people like Nick and Seamus find it funny, and that people like me find it tawdry, cheap, easy, and unfunny. More to the point, I am expected to be outraged, which is an essential part of what makes it funny. But I don't. I just find it tired and pointless.

"This is the kind of stuff that is supposed to polarise people. I'm supposed to either be outraged by it or love it because of the way it outrages other people. It's not funny, it's just provocative. And the problem is that I don't really want to be on either side of that game, so I just don't react." They more or less gave up trying after that, thankfully, although I did still have to listen to it over and over again in the van. I think it was a kind of therapy for them. It helped them make sure that the numbness hadn't completely taken over. Like cigarette burns on the arm. If Neil Hamburger still got to you on some level, then you hadn't completely lost your grip.

Neil Hamburger is the reason why the band's GPS got nicknamed "Julia." The voice used to speak the driving instructions was female. At some point it was issuing commands in it's eerily neutral tone of voice and presumably at the same moment Neil Hamburger was telling a "joke" about Julia Roberts. The connection was made and from then on "Julia" was either the target of derision or a valued part of the entourage. Just like all the human inhabitants of the van I suppose.

We arrived in Chepstow and checked out the venue – a small, black hall behind a pub with a basic stage at the end. There was also something that

I took to be a stripper pole nailed to a wooden platform that shifted around a corner near the stage. I never got around to asking about that. The venue was a spartan affair, but it had more of the feel of a Vancouver venue than Bristol or Plymouth. The crowd was a mix of non-descript locals, some local colour, and some of the Bristol crowd who came out to see the band again, including Kev and Zoey. In the pub, Seamus, Nick and Kev started talking about Neil Hamburger again – Kev had become a convert. Nick made a crack about how Zoey probably found it distasteful and wished she had someone else to talk to. She turned to me and changed the subject. No one else seemed to pick up on her clear but hopelessly subtle message.

The boys were delighted to see the Bristol contingent again and make new friends with the Chepstow locals. Everyone stood around the pub and its outside patio, chatting and socialising. Whatever performance anxiety may have been going on with the band members was so slight as to be unnoticeable. They would never hide or fuss before going on stage. More often than not they could be found in the front of the crowd during the opening bands' sets, moshing and jumping around with everyone else. In the time-honoured tradition of folk music, to which punk owes many unacknowledged debts, a Dreadnoughts show was as much about socialising as it was about music, and the barrier between the stage and the audience was often blurred to the the point of being invisible.

Inside the venue before the show I found Nick in an odd mood. I offered to help put up the banner and he brushed me aside. I got increasingly spooked when a casual comment from me concerning how the lighting might be arranged got misinterpreted as a command from the band, and one which Nick disagreed with. For the first time I started to feel conspicuously out of step with things and it was an uncomfortable place to be. I started to question exactly what my role was. I had always assumed that my help with the support tasks – moving heavy gear, setting up the banner, checking to make sure everything was working – would be welcome. But something about my behaviour seemed to be getting on their nerves. Perhaps it was me. Perhaps it was just a general edginess. I was the only one of the six of us that they could live without, so there was little risk in putting me in a boat and giving it a shove. The touring malaise was hitting me now, and I started to back off and try to give the situation some space.

The question often crossed my mind of whether I was an observer or a participant. Of course the reality is that I was a bit of both. I was an outsider, not part of the band, and clearly on the outside when I was taking pictures. But I inevitably became part of the traveling gong show in every way except the stage. I tried never to lead, but always to be somewhere in the middle. Perhaps that was too much. Being always "in the middle" seems like a benign thing, but it also means that you are always there. No one ever gets a break from you. Sometimes you need to risk missing out on a defining moment so that you don't alienate the people around you.

After the show we were shown our accommodations. It was a disused B&B connected upstairs from the pub. Marco was ecstatic. "Look at this place, it's awesome." Internally I responded "No it isn't. Its squalid and filthy." Abandoned food littered the table and the bedrooms were little more than storage for stacks of old mattresses. It was one of those places that didn't seem to have a right angle anywhere in sight. I don't think it had been a functioning, hospitable B&B for some time.

Filth, it seems to me, is a relative quality. Over the years I've seen such a broad range of what is considered acceptable. I've seen the middle class suburban homes that keep plastic on the lampshades to try to preserve their just-bought look. I've gone to see potential apartments where there was frost on the ceiling and two month old dishes in the sink. We all seem to have our own definition of what is tolerable, and beyond that, what constitutes a health risk. For young men that bar is typically incredibly low. So in hindsight it wasn't too surprising that Marco thought this place was "awesome." It had walls, a (mostly functional) bathroom, they didn't need to share it with anyone else, and it was free. As a general rule, young men don't seek out quality and splendour for their living spaces, they just want a fort that they can play in.

In one of the small rooms I piled my bags on top of the stack of mattresses after pulling the top mattress off and laying it on the empty bedframe. Then I wandered into what served as a living room and settled in to write up my notes. Outside the window, one storey above the pavement in front of the pub, I heard voices. Someone was talking to Drew and Seamus, undoubtedly about their experience with Andrew.

"He's probably one of the scariest people I've ever seen in my life, and then I met him and he's probably one of the nicest people I've ever met."

By 0200h it was reported that Andrew was in the van, sleeping. Nick had, theoretically, gone to bed and Marco was in the hall skyping with his girlfriend. Drew and Seamus were still outside, talking loudly and drinking with the locals. Their voices disappeared from the conversation at some point and I heard someone say that they'd gone off to a party.

I went to bed. Fully dressed and using my dreads for a pillow. Sometimes there's just no point in pretending.

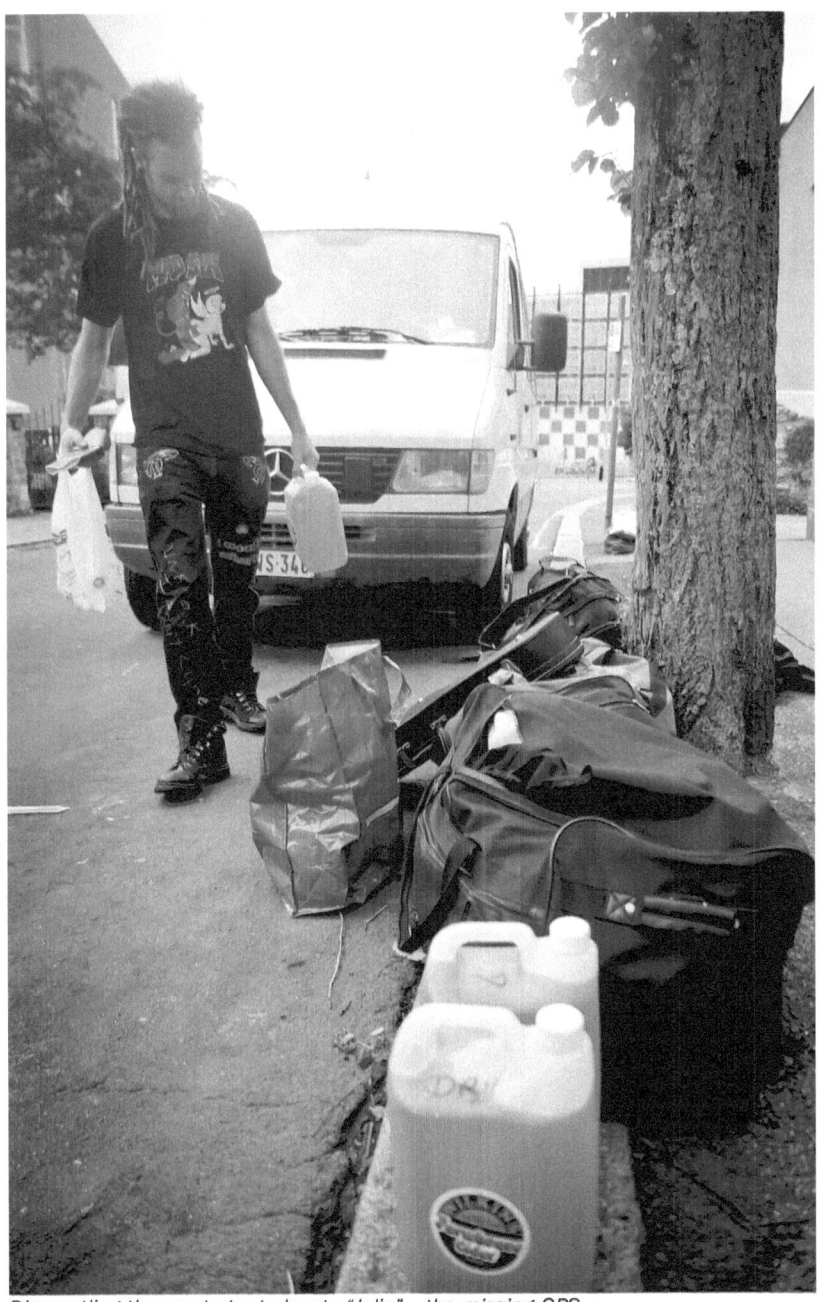

Dismantling the van to try to locate "Julia" – the missing GPS.

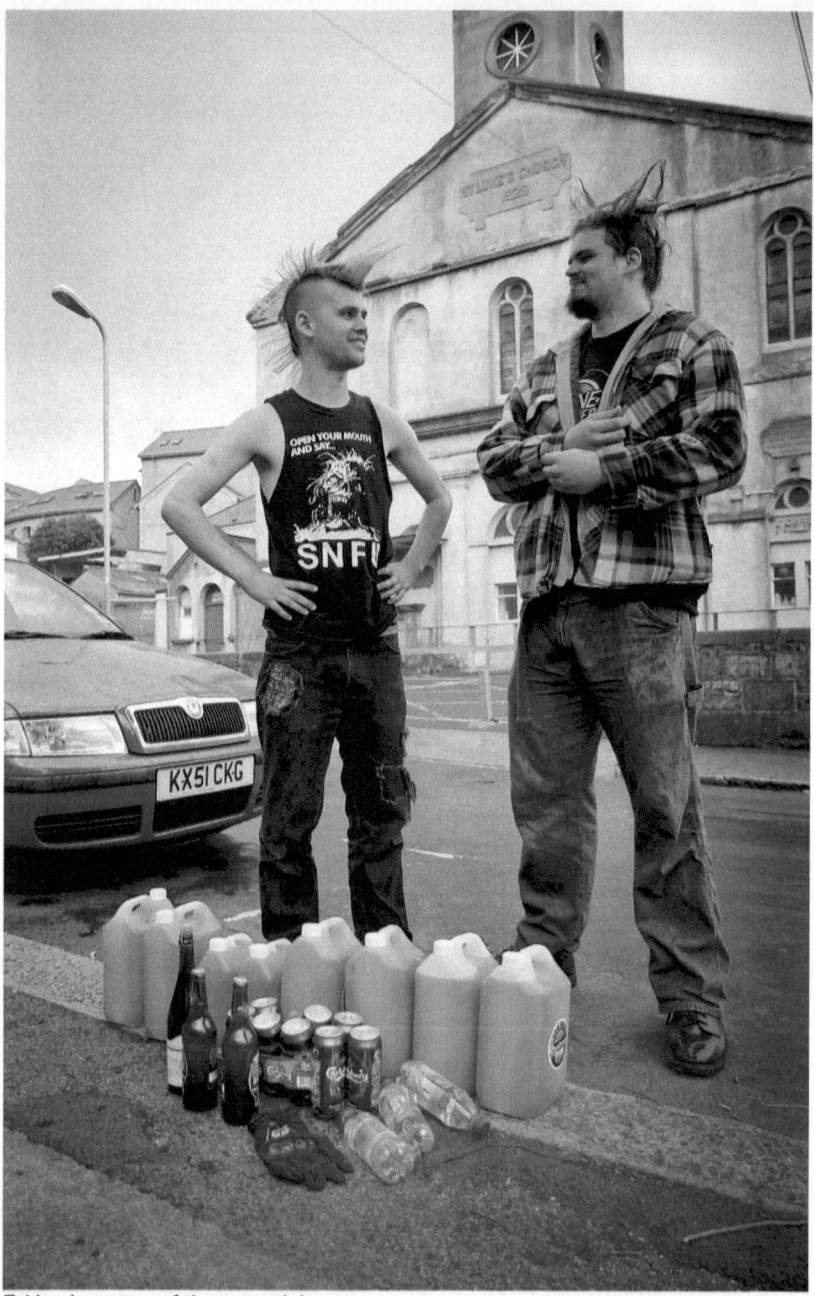

Taking inventory of the essentials.

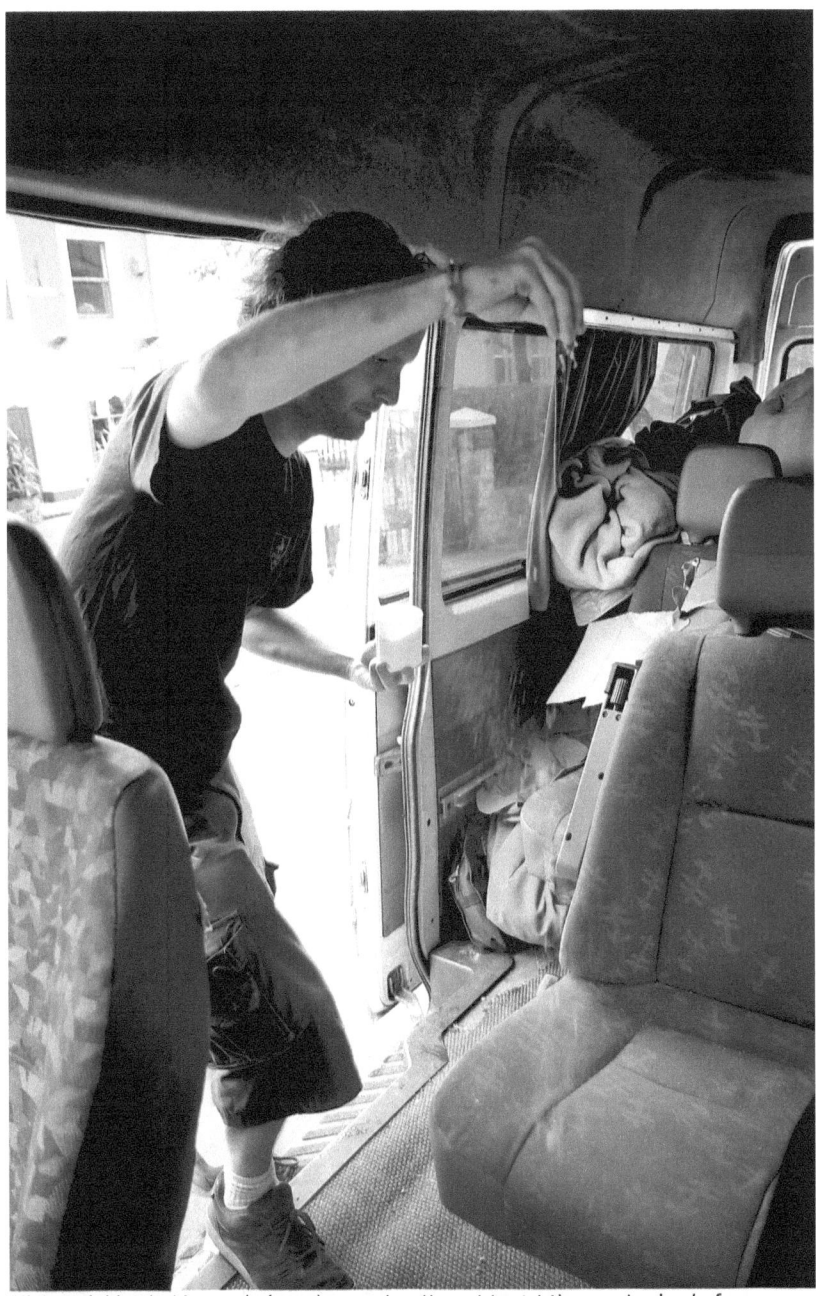

Nick sprinkles baking soda in a desperate attempt to get the van to rise before baking.

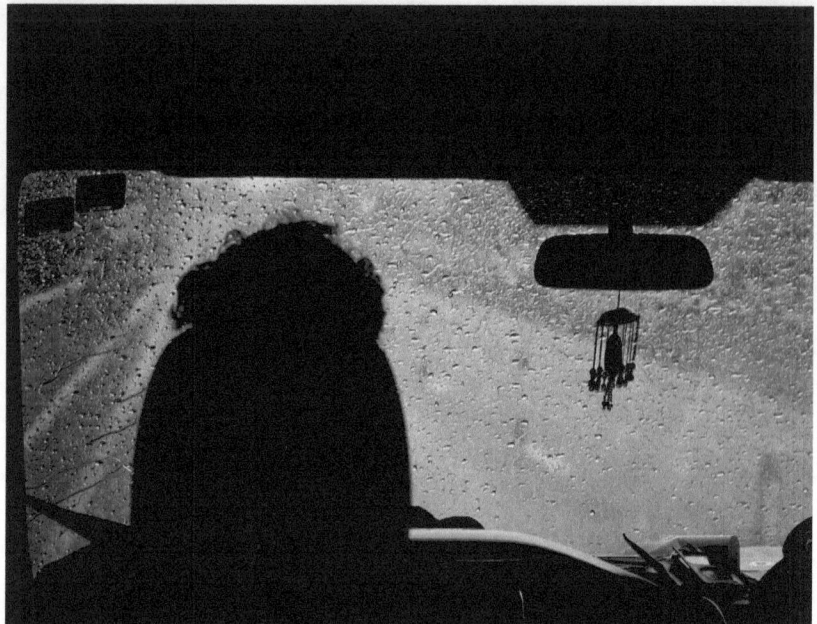

Marco drives on to Chepstow through a light rain. The van is probably going about 120 kmph in this photo. He's able to drive because the visual hallucinations of his dementia are thankfully exactly the opposite of the rain on the windshield, canceling each other out.

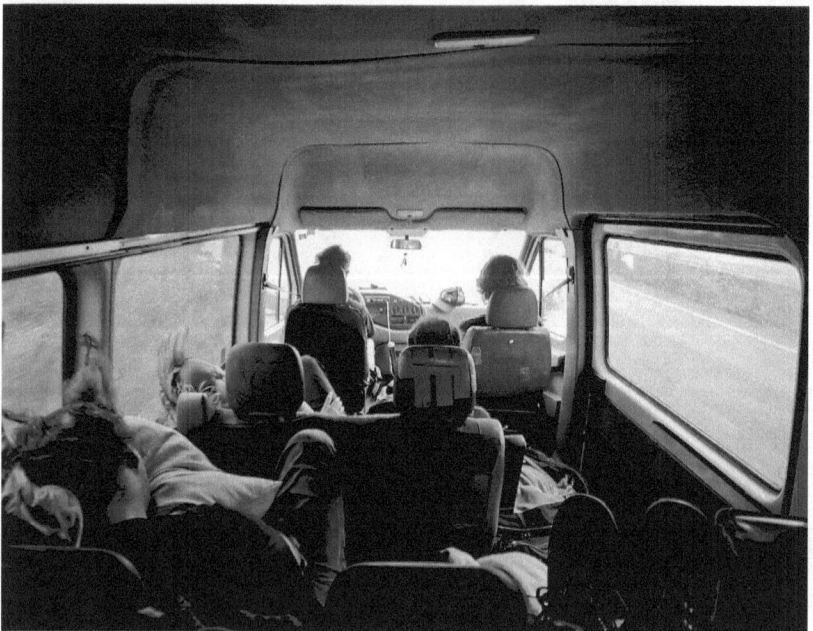

The van interior, as seen from the sleeping bunk at the back.

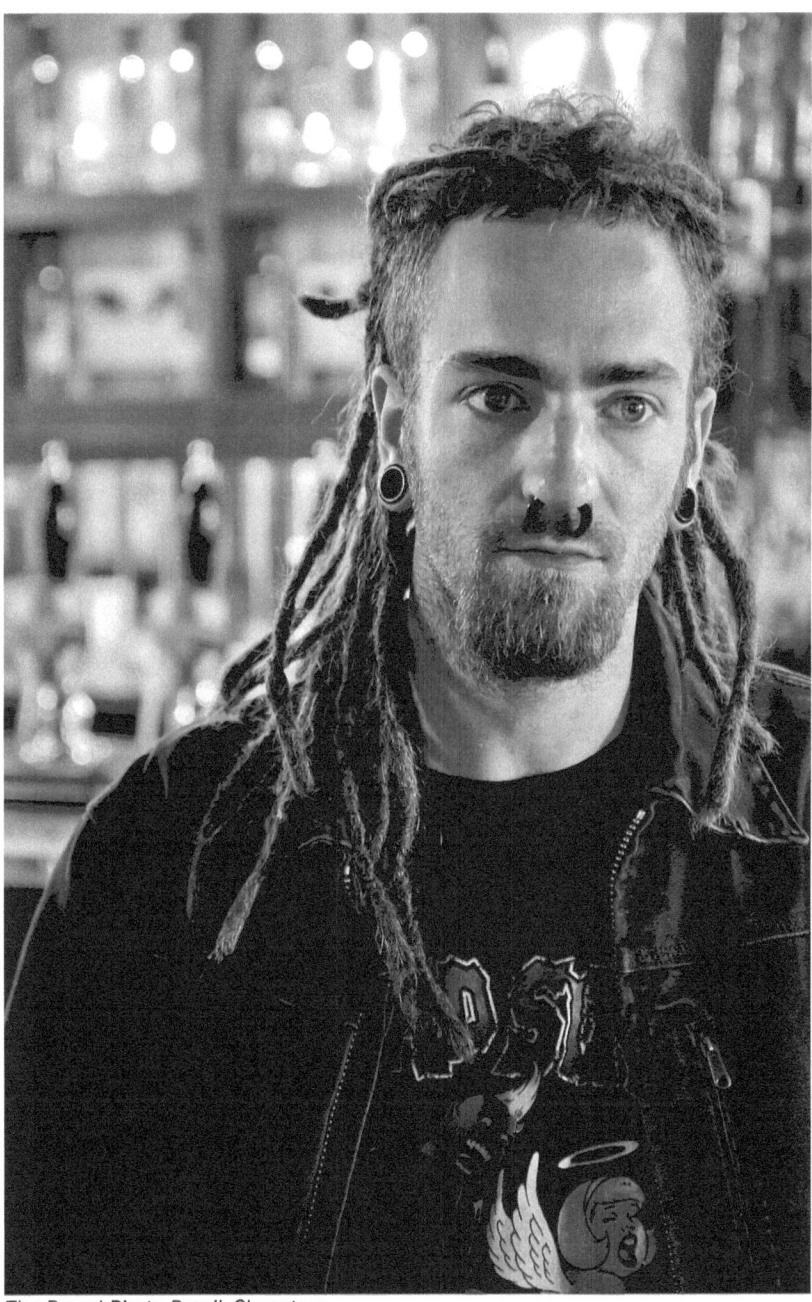

The Dread Pirate Druzil, Chepstow.

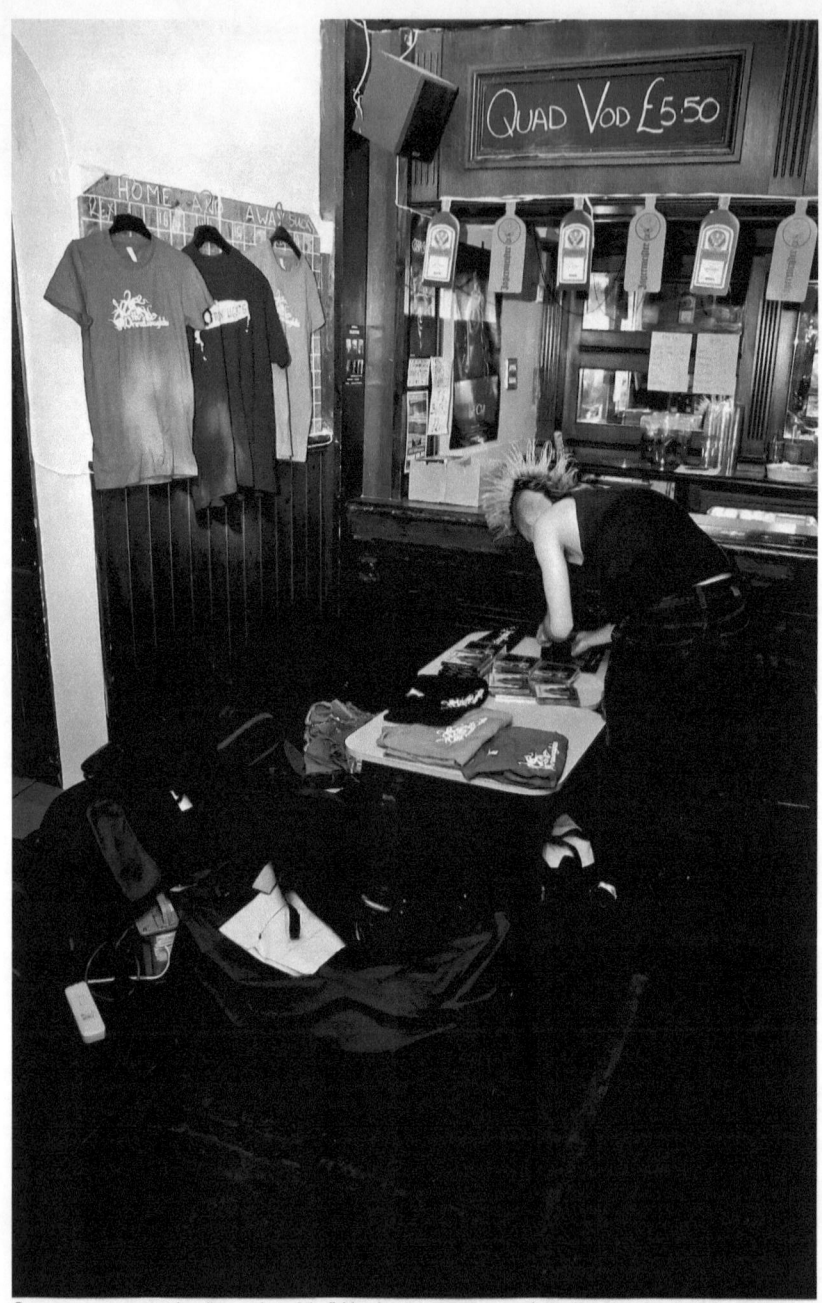

Seamus sets up the "merch table." Having decent merchandise is absolutely critical. It keeps cash flowing while on the road. A "Quad Vod" is not a local Welsh brew, it's four shots of vodka – widely recognised as a way to get extremely drunk, extremely quickly.

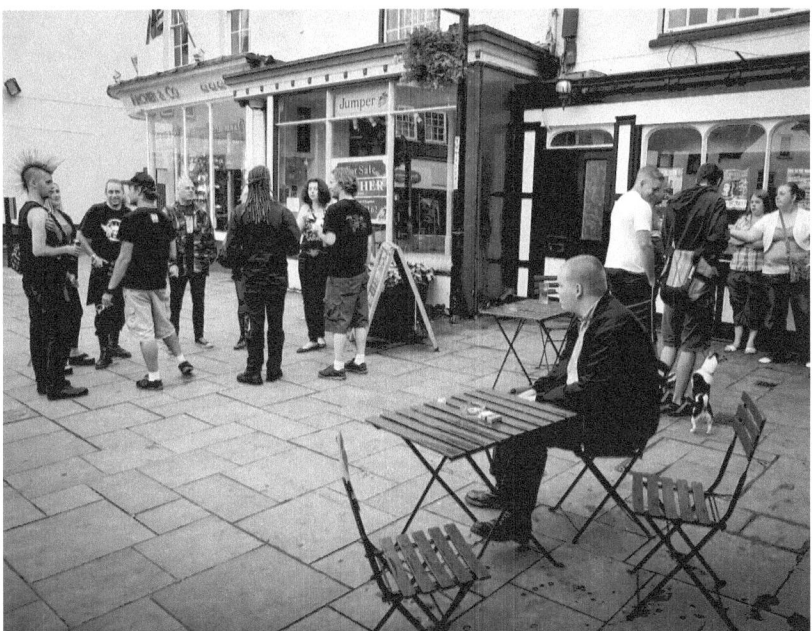
The band socializes with fans before the show with fans. Many had followed them from Bristol.

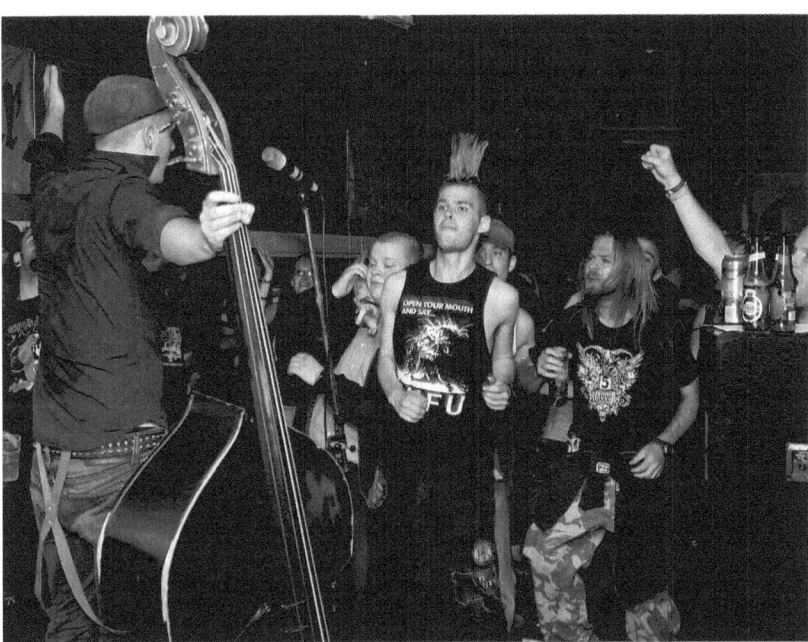
Drew, Seamus, and Nick can all be picked out from the front of the opening act's set. They consistently show enthusiastic support for the bands they play with.

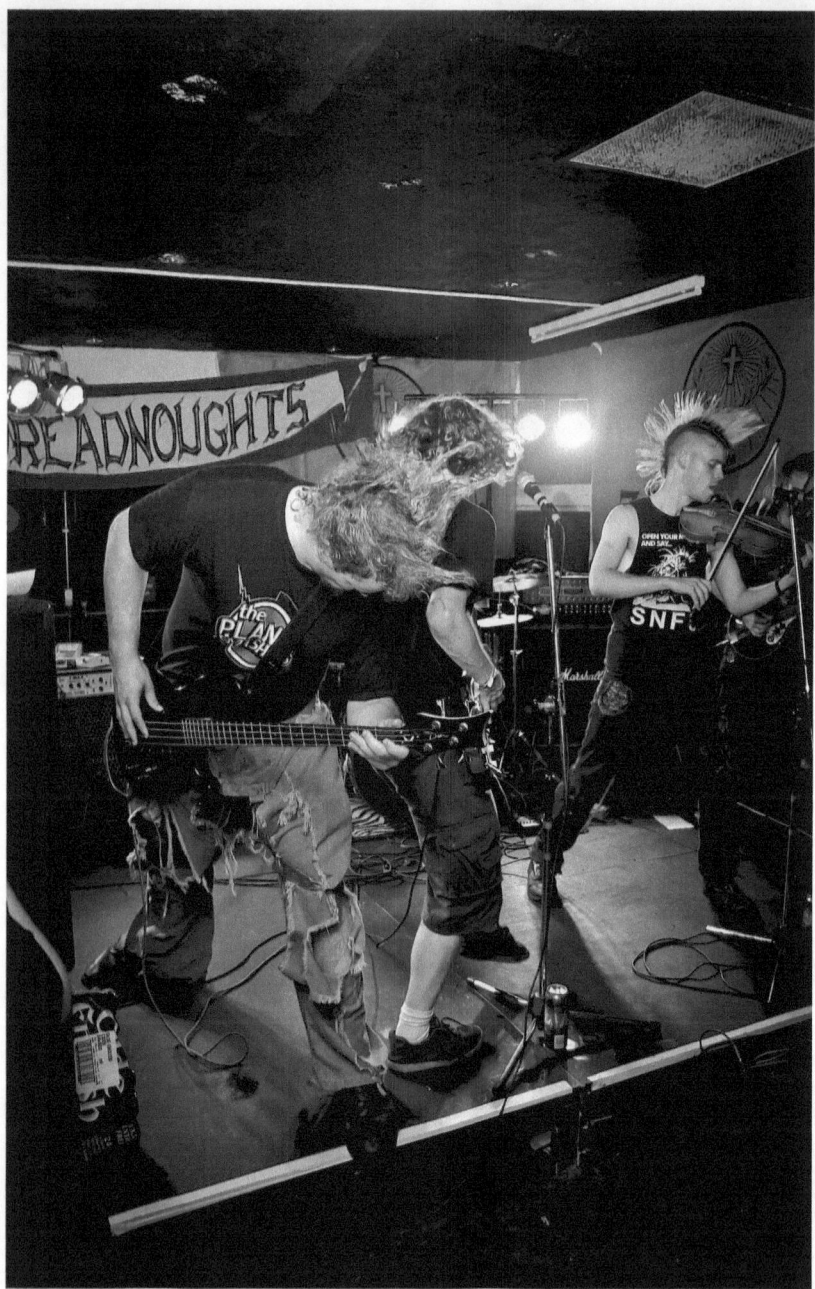

Perhaps one day, if the fates are kind, the band will be able to land one of those lucrative pant company sponsorships.

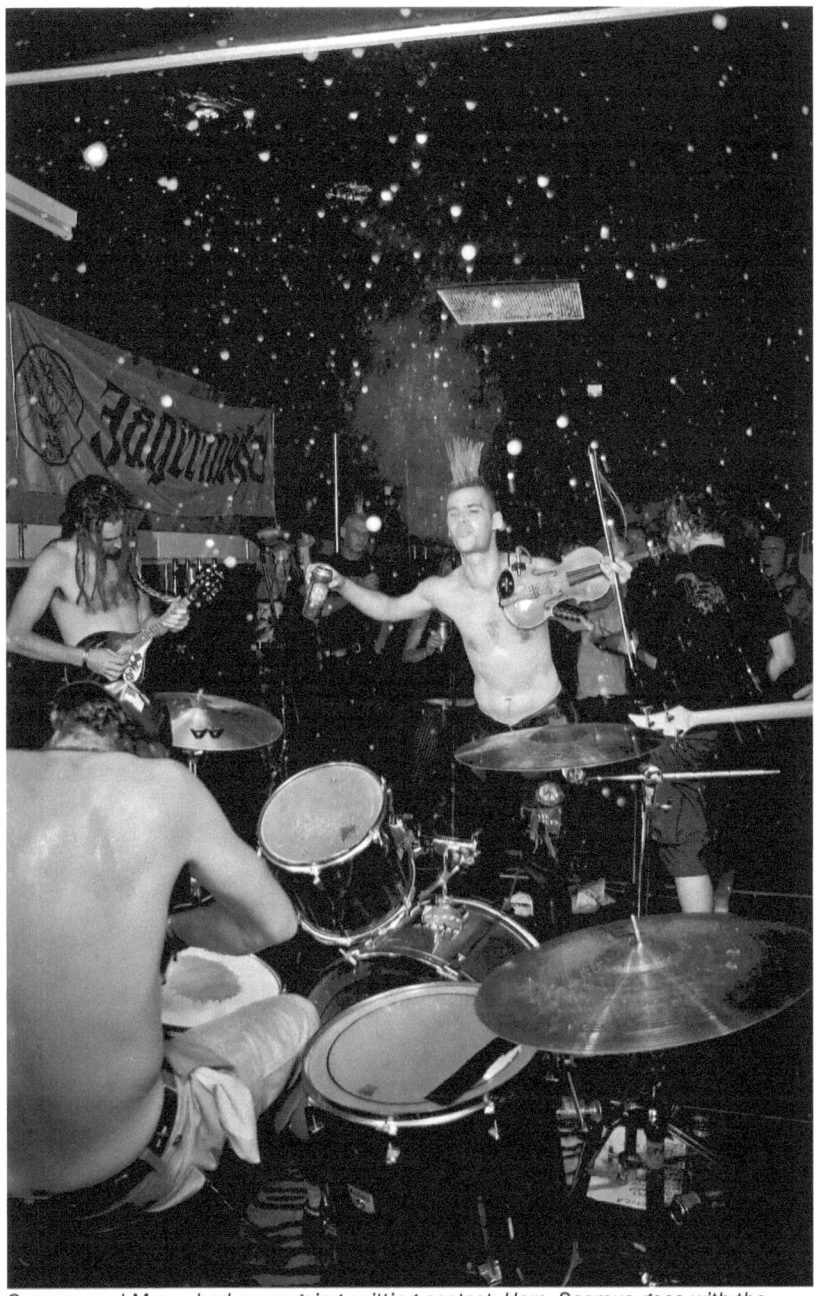

Seamus and Marco had an ongoing spitting contest. Here, Seamus goes with the "nuclear option," spraying Marco with a mouthful of cider.

This Place Is Awesome

YOU REALLY SHOULD DO SOMETHING ABOUT THE TRAMPS.

Day Four
July 4 – Chepstow, Stoke on Trent.

The next morning I wandered downstairs to find that Drew and Seamus had, in a fit of drunken bravado, decided to try to scale the wall of the local castle at four in the morning after eating a bunch of morning glory flowers under the mistaken belief that they could get high from them. It hadn't occurred to them that this was a castle. The whole point of the place was that you couldn't get in that way. It's probably a good thing that they gave up quickly because on the other side of the castle was a tall cliff that dropped directly into the River Wye. I'm sure some kind of diving competition might have been contemplated if they hadn't decided instead to just curl up at the foot of the current wall and fall asleep.

They were woken that morning by a school child looking down on them from above.

"Mummy, are those tramps down there? Why are there tramps sleeping outside the castle?"

"Those aren't tramps, they're just dummies."

"No, they're tramps. I heard them talking to each other."

Somehow the six of us managed to find each other and the hunt for breakfast in the small, sleepy town began. The Beaufort Hotel, it turns out, makes the most sublime Welsh Rarebit I have ever tasted. (I emailed them later and begged for the recipe, but never heard back.) The secret ingredient, I came to understand, was a not inconsiderable amount of Guinness. I wasn't the only person for whom Guinness was a part of their breakfast, but in Drew's case it was a full pint in a glass and not just one ingredient in a larger meal. Starting the day with a pint of Guinness seemed like a sure prescription for a stunning case of the logies before noon.

We returned to the castle after breakfast to take some pictures of the band. I had been to this particular castle many years before on a trip to Wales and was eager to photograph the band in what I knew to be a great location. Sadly the exhibit of medieval armour that the public was invited to try on was undergoing renovations, but we found lots of other good places for pictures on the grounds. A full gallon jug of Wilkins cider can be seen in some of the photos. It was a constant companion. As we were leaving the gift shop the band saw fit to leave humourous comments in the guest book, including an exhortation to "do something about the tramps." One day I have to get back there and see if the page is still in the book.

We piled back into the van and turned towards for Stoke.

In Stoke the band played their first empty house. It was a classic fuck up and the band had nothing to do with the almost perfect failure that resulted. A show was added at the last minute in a small city in the Midlands. It was a Monday night and not only was the name of the venue wrong, but when we found the right venue it turned out that they didn't normally do bands on Mondays. The band did the right thing – with the obliviousness that is the blessing of any worker bee, they set up, soundchecked, and played a full set to an audience of four staff and three patrons. To their credit they played with vigour and humour. They didn't bring their "A" game, but their "B" game is better than many bands' best, and I don't think they even have a "C" level show.

And in that odd little bar in the middle of nowhere, with only three audience members, they managed to hook up with two of them and get free accommodations out of the third. It's not quite the same as finding out that the third free wish you are being granted can indeed be "can I have three more wishes?," but it was as close as I can imagine.

We packed up the gear and drove to Thom's flat, which was miraculously spacious and clean. Thom was a student and the flat was normally shared with other students and featured at least four proper bedrooms with real beds. This being summer it was empty of roommates who might be bothered by six drunken Canadians who wanted to stay up all night playing music. We sat around the living room, drinking cider, playing music, and looking at some of the photographs I'd taken up to that point. Some time around 0500h it was all starting to wind down and I headed for the bedroom that I'd staked out earlier. One of the band members intercepted me and asked if he could have that room. Not being much of a "guy's guy," I don't often run into those situations where one male makes a request of another in a way that makes it clear that the request is not something that can be turned down. Not in a Godfather, "an offer you can't refuse" kind of way, but in more of an "unwritten rule about male priorities" kind of way. This particular band member's choice of room had been already been claimed, and he was "in need of a double occupancy room," as he put it.

I still had most of my respect and affection for these guys intact at that point, and there was a decent couch in the living room, so I did my male duty and gave up the room so that he might have his tryst. Never let it be said that I got in the way of true love. Or a quickie. Either way. I grabbed my bags and headed back to the living room.

To correctly set the stage for the next story I need to flashback to Bristol for a moment and the Reckless Engineer. Imagine Marco, a couple of hours before the show, walking around the club holding a laptop at the end of his outstretched arms.

Marco had been smitten by a girl he met in Saskatoon, barely a week into a tour that would take him to the other side of the world for two months. Once again the drummer proves to have the most peculiar sense of timing. He spent much of the time that I was with the band "Skyping" with her. Any time Marco was missing it was a pretty safe bet you'd find him in the vicinity of the nearest free WiFi connection. On the one hand this kept him out of trouble and limited his drinking a little, which was important as he was the only one capable of driving the van. But it also placed him outside of the group, socially. Sometimes this is a good thing. Sometimes it isn't.

In Bristol, Marco had seized the opportunity to use the free WiFi at the venue to give his new love a tour of the place. It seemed a bit pointless. It was not the kind of place that would defy description. Or even benefit from it, for that matter.

Back to Stoke now, where Marco's Skyping habits played a key role in one of the defining moments for me. There were only two times I was really concerned for my safety. And only one time did I put my foot down and do something about it.

I had settled into the couch just as the last of the stragglers left to crash for a few hours. All but one. It was 0530h and Marco had been quietly Skyping with his little Saskatoon berry since early in the evening, and was now fully engaged in a video chat with her. In an act of perceived courtesy, he switched to earphones so that he wouldn't disturb me while I slept. I'm sure that was the theory.

And so it was, in that featureless room, strewn with musical instruments, mismatched furniture, lace up sneakers covered in tiny skulls, and various empty bottles, with the morning sun now well established in the window, that I was woken for the millionth time by a flurry of typing and entirely audible sniggering, as he and his far flung fling shared another private joke. It was at this point that I realised that every time I'd been woken up, I'd looked across the room to see him swigging from a jug of potent West Country cider.

It was closing in on 0600h and this guy had literally been drinking all night – and, mathematically-speaking, half of the morning too. Some time possibly before noon he had to climb behind the wheel of the van and be sober and awake enough to drive us all to Newcastle. He wasn't showing any signs of slowing down or falling asleep. This seemed like a set up for an incredibly stupid and avoidable death, so I propped myself up on one elbow and said "Marco, you need to stop drinking. NOW." To his credit, he did. I'm not sure what time he finally closed the lid on the laptop and slept. Or where.

Perhaps there's a physiologist out there who can explain to me how a 20-something male body can do all that and bounce back faster than

Superman returning a high lob, but I swear to god I was watching him like a hawk as he drove and he was alert and in control the whole time. Well... by "in control" I mean his reaction time and coordination was perfectly normal. His judgement was arguably impaired, but that was because he's Marco, not because he had been drinking. His judgement is always a bit suspect.

I talked to Nick about the attitude towards drinking that existed within the band. "Medium functioning alcoholism – that's what it is. One day it will degenerate into low functioning alcoholism." It was a cynical view. Nick is the keeper of the band cynicism. But rock and roll has a well earned reputation for treating its practitioners in a callous and cynical way. It's a world in which medium functioning alcoholics can thrive, and low functioning alcoholics can survive without having to face themselves in any meaningful way. Being a fuck up is romanticised. These guys aren't true fuck ups though. They play at being fuck ups. The question I frequently find myself asking is "will they be able to make the transition out of the 'lovable fuck up' personas when the time comes for them to turn pro? Or might they even be able to do that most impressive of magic tricks – creating the illusion of the fuck up personality, while living a secret life of professionalism, comfort, and sobriety?"

I guess in the end I managed at least a couple of hours of fitful sleep on that couch. It certainly could have been worse. And in a few days, it was.

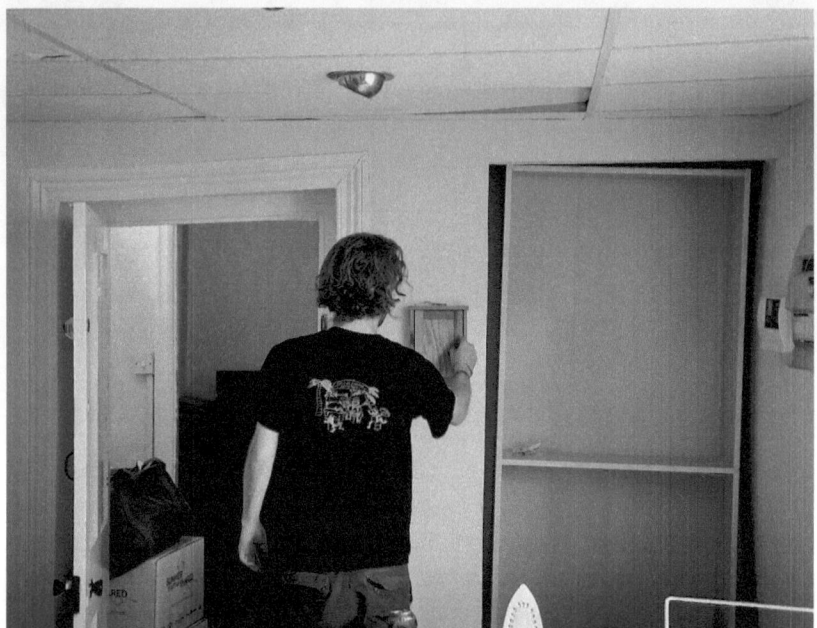

This is not an optical illusion. Nick attempts to straighten a frame, but it's unclear what it is he's using as a reference point.

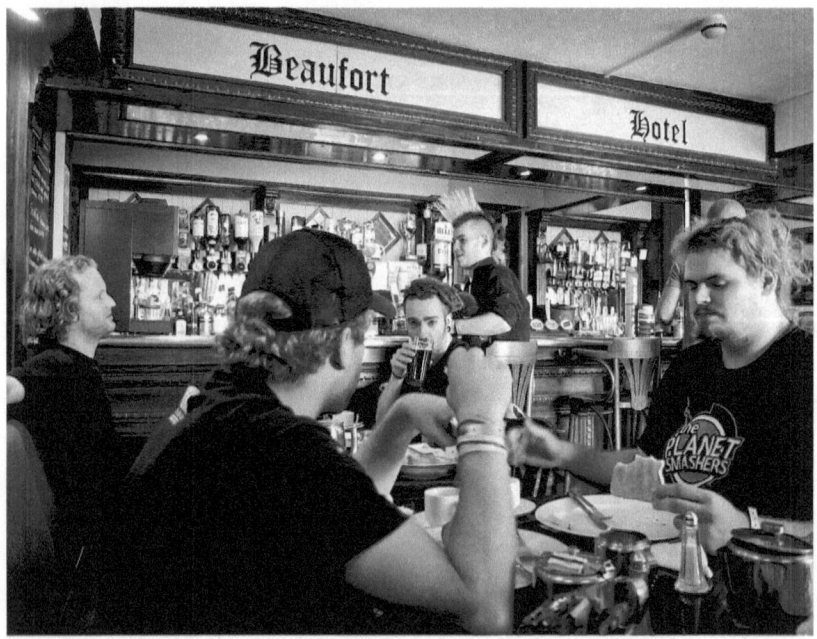

Breakfast in Chepstow. A traditional British breakfast accompanied by tea and Guinness.

This Place Is Awesome

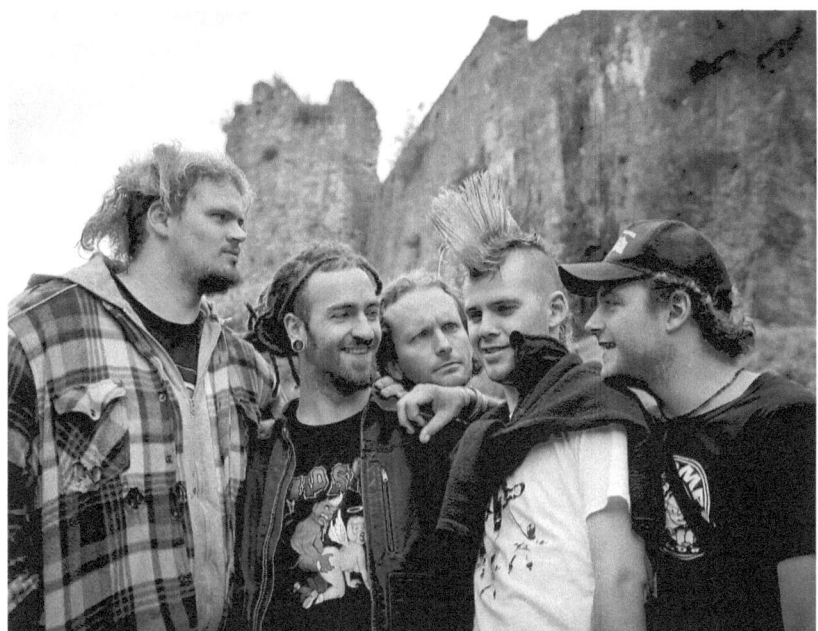

The boys outside Chepstow Castle. In the background is Drew and Seamus's previous night's accommodations.

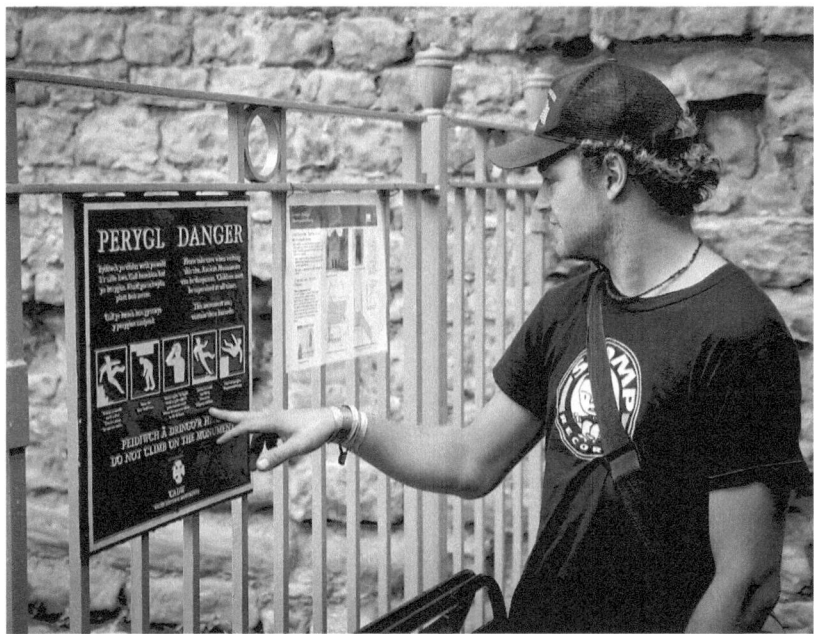

Marco checks out all the ways that he might die while exploring the castle.

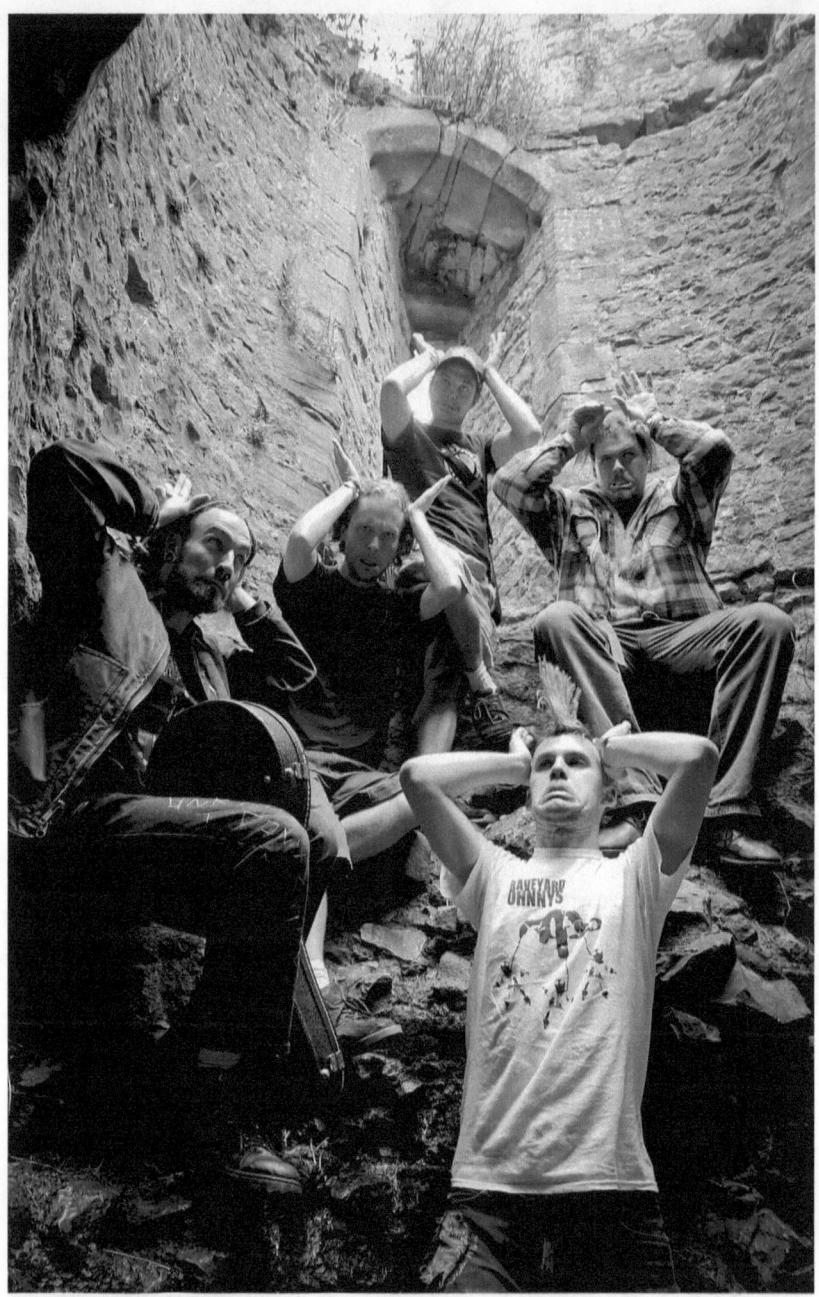

Seamus directs a photo shoot in the castle: everyone doing a "llama"

　　　　　　　This Place Is Awesome

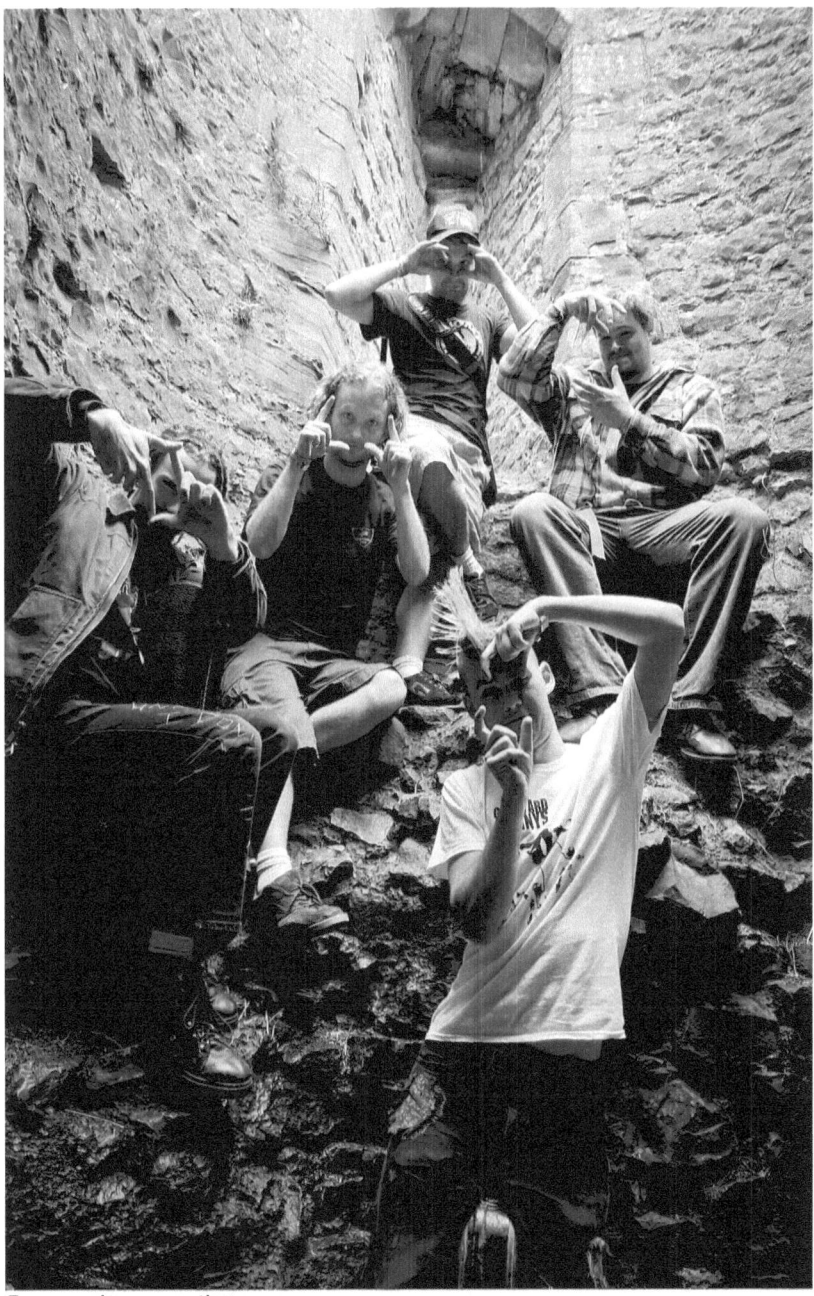

Everyone impersonating me.

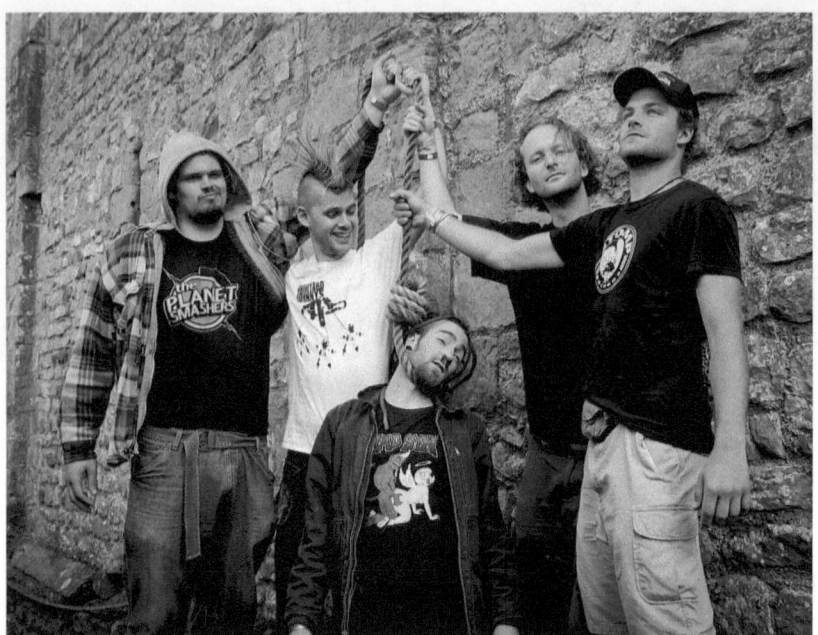

Drew pays the inevitable price for smoking in the van.

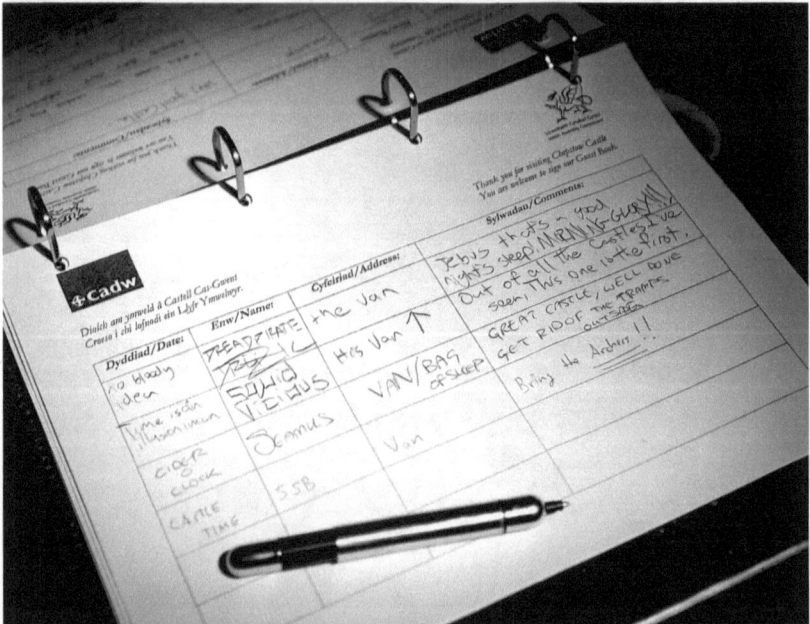

The guest book at Chepstow Castle. Perhaps one day this page will be valuable.

This Place Is Awesome

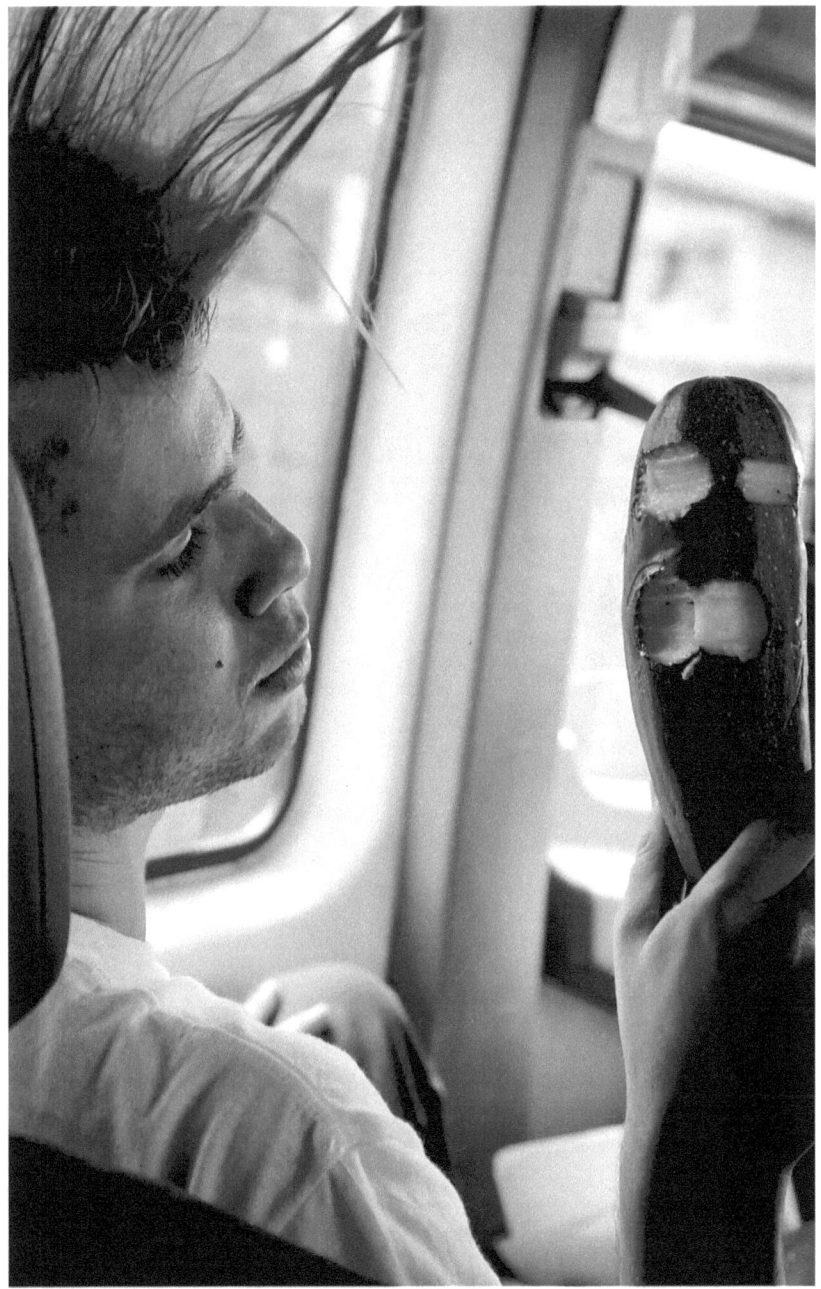

On the way to Stoke. Seamus makes a new friend.

This Place Is Awesome

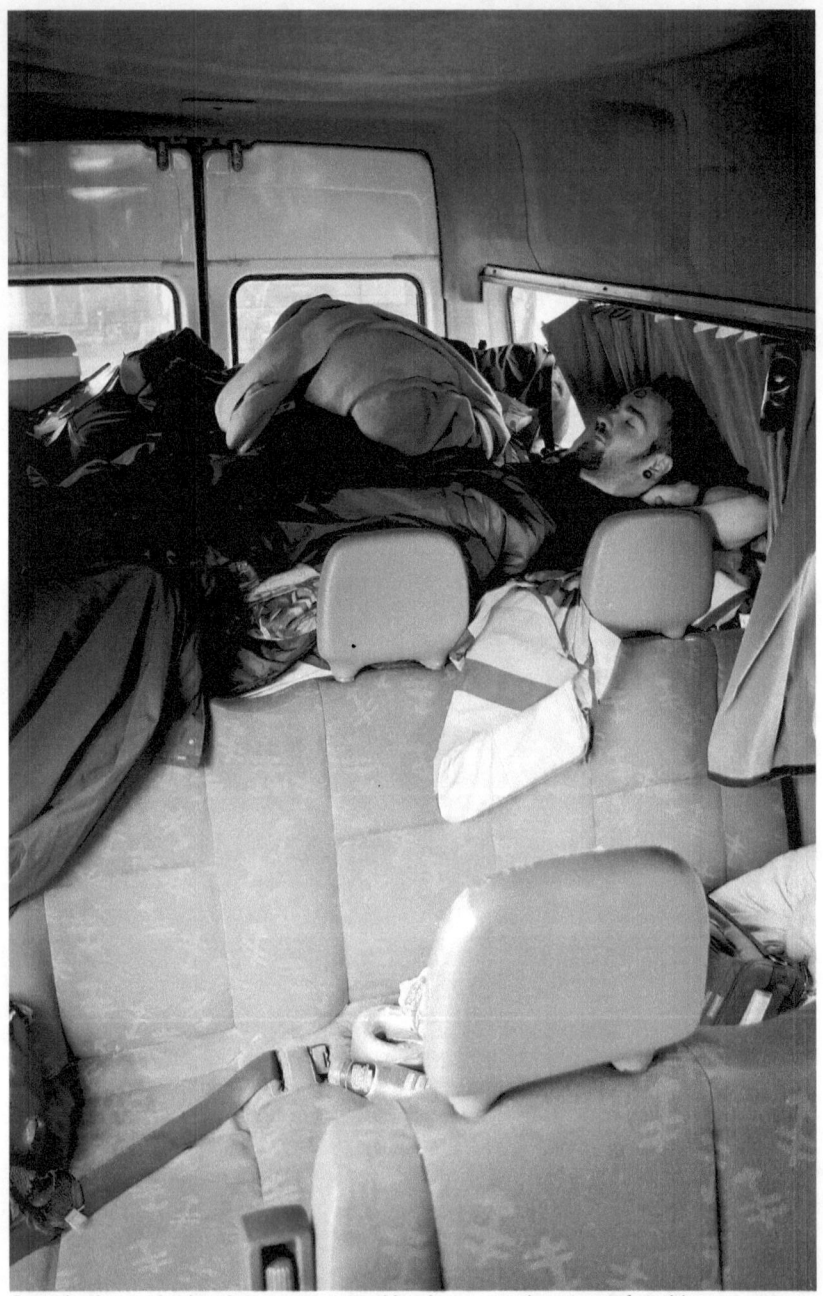

Drew in the van's sleeping quarters, making it seems almost comfortable.

This Place Is Awesome

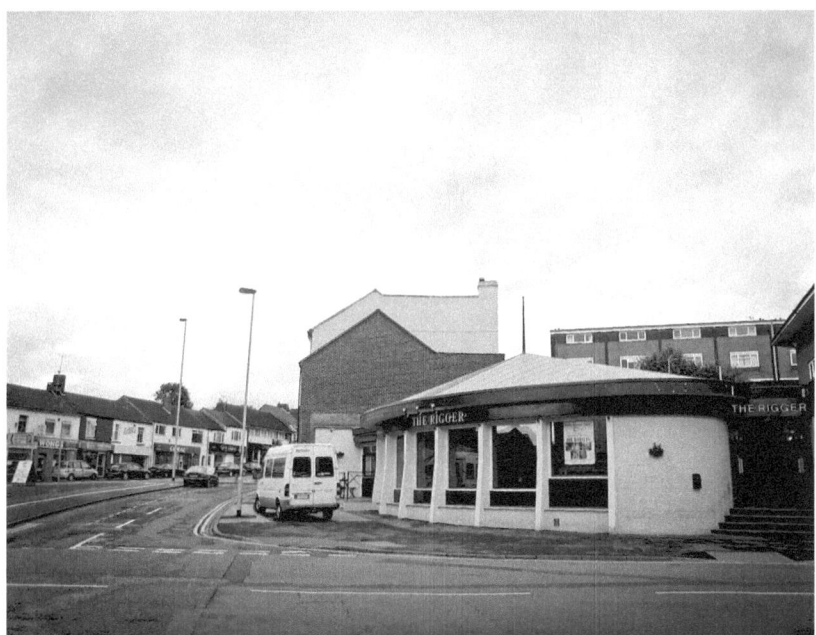

The tour van parked in front of The Rigger in Stoke. Note the lack of humans anywhere. Not generally a good omen for a nightclub.

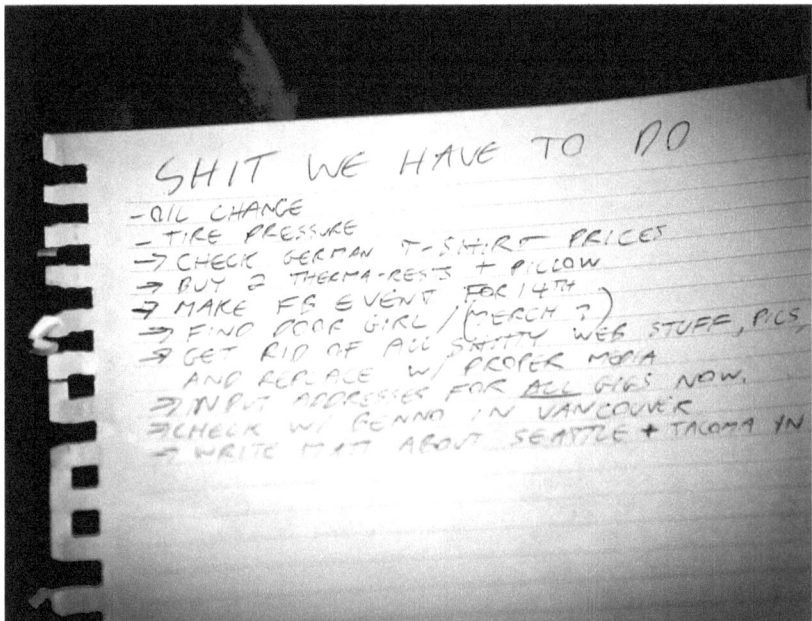

I think they're still waiting to get the oil changed.

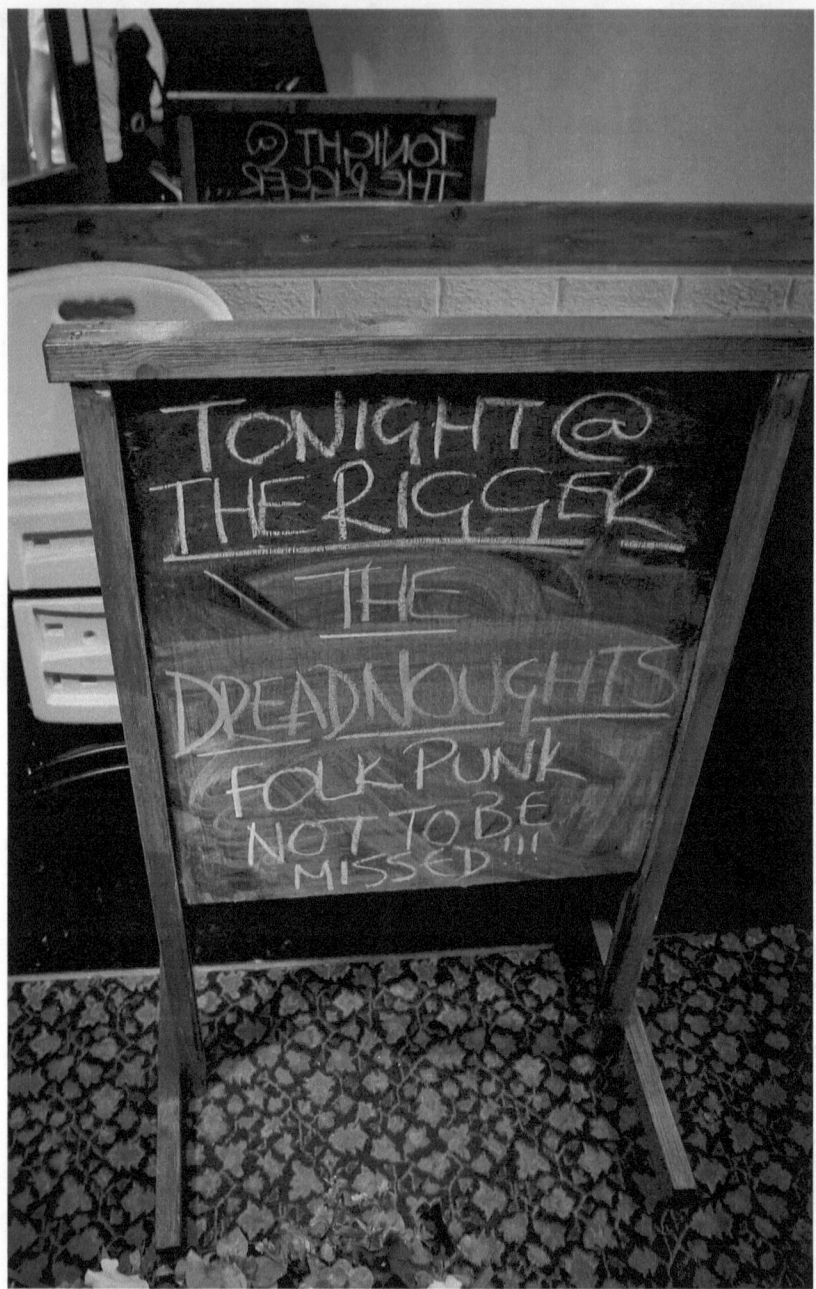

"Not to be missed." Big irony win.

This Place Is Awesome

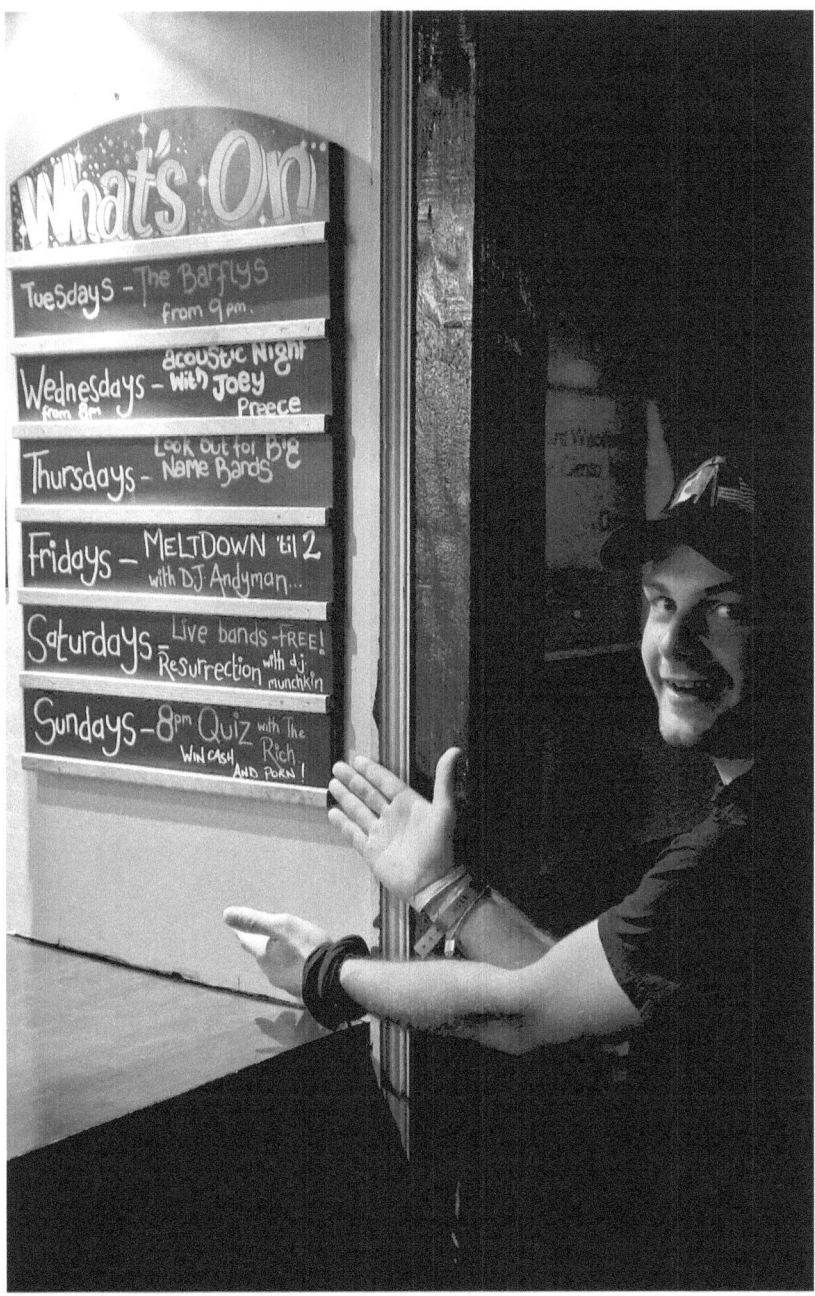

"Sundays – 8PM Quiz. Win cash and porn!"
Also note that the sign does not list Mondays at all. Guess what night this was.

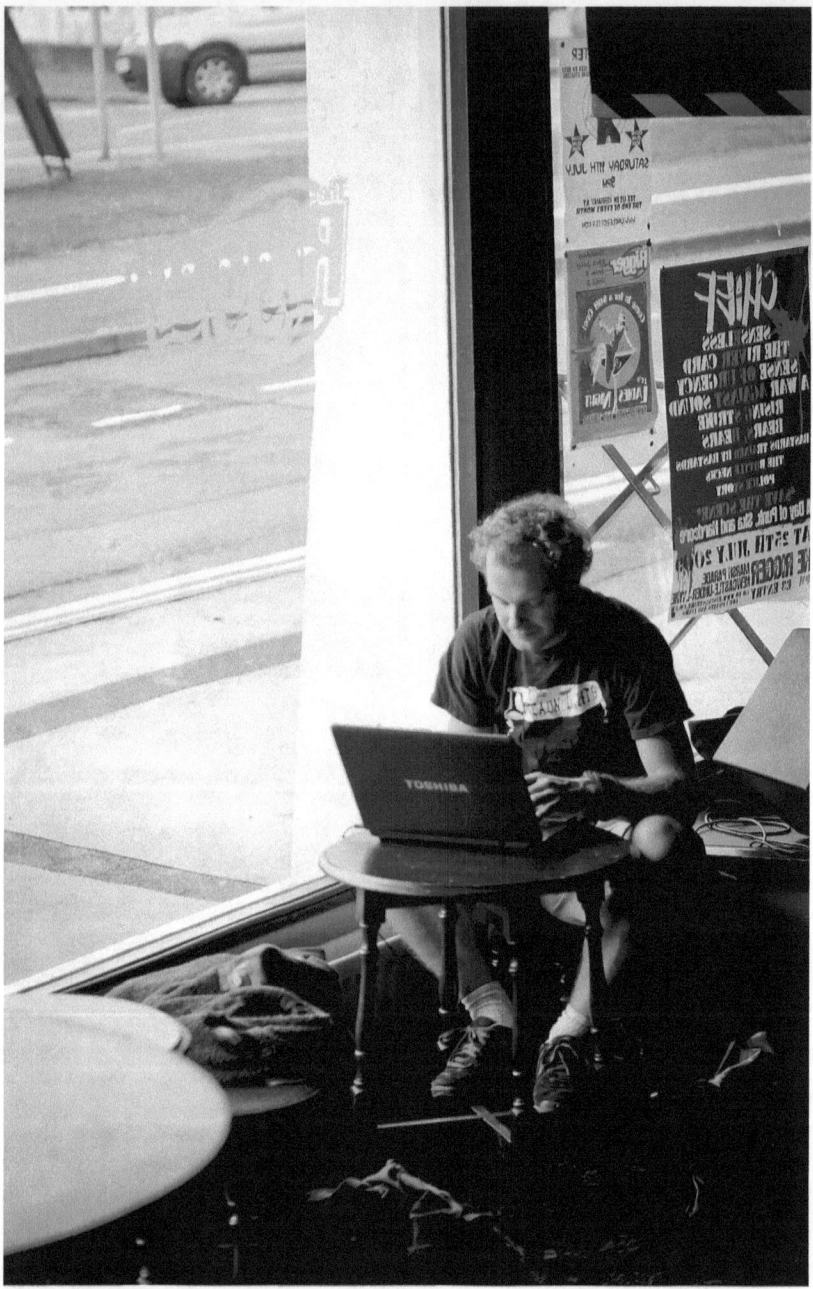

Marco Skyping... again.

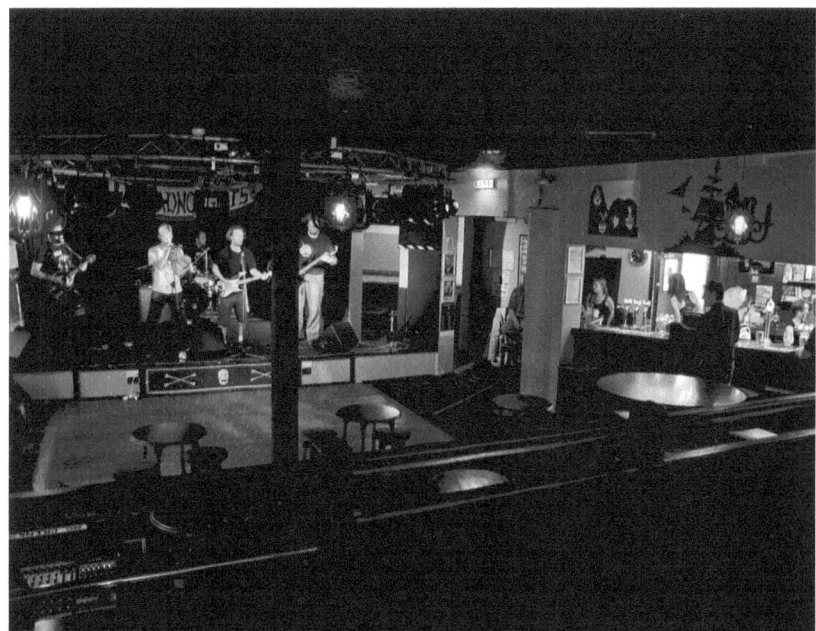

Playing to an empty house in Stoke. Actually, the entire audience can be seen on the right side of the photo. Every band goes through at least one of these shows.

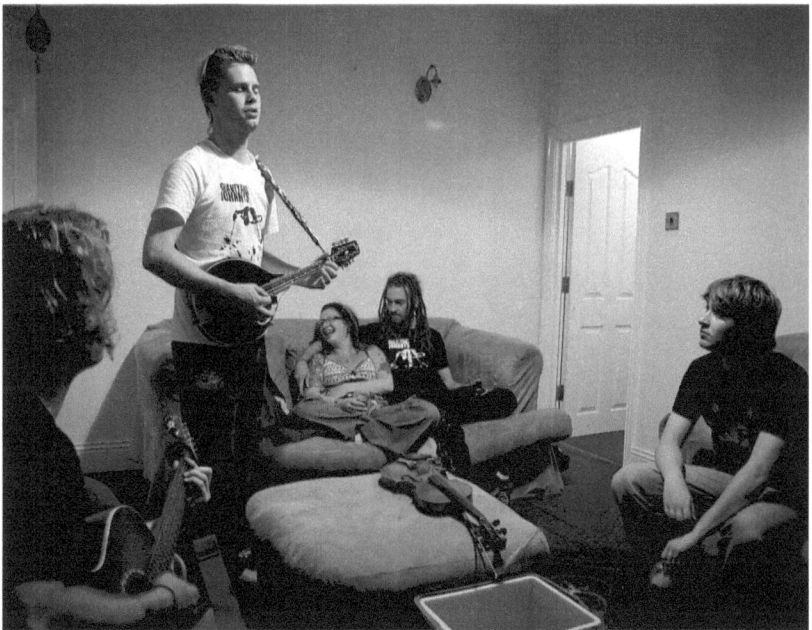

0100h – Back at Thom's flat, the music continues late into the night.

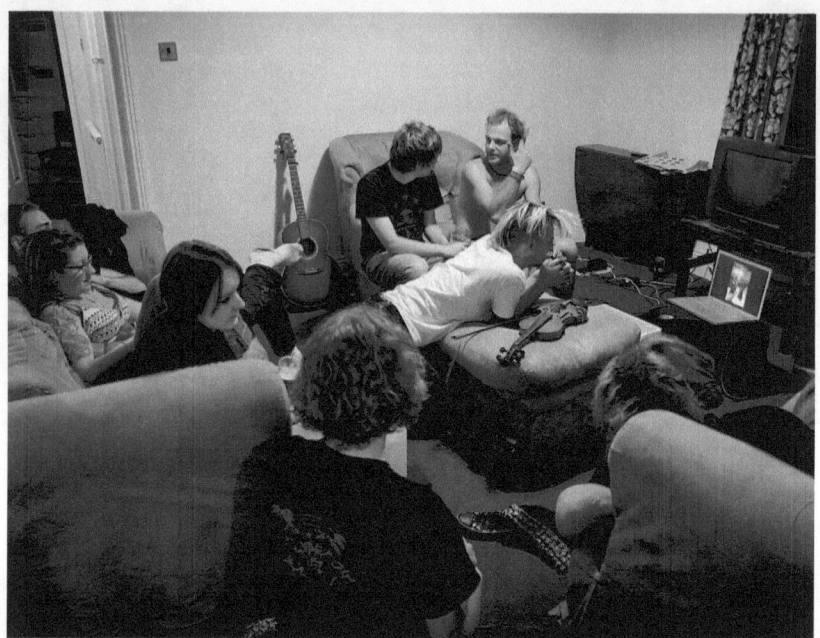

0300h – An impromptu slideshow of photos from the previous few days.

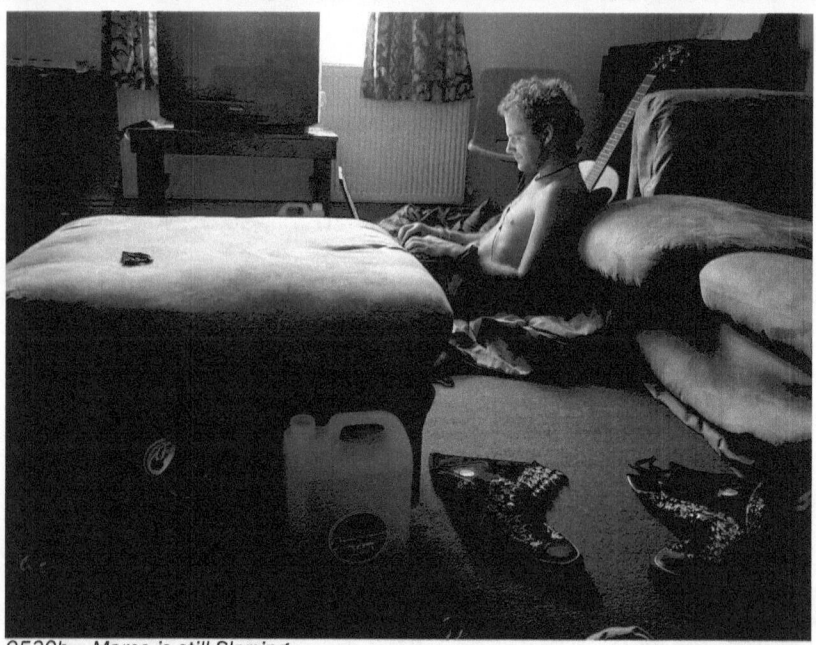

0530h – Marco is still Skyping.

IS THAT
THE BEST
YOU CAN DO,
YOU PUSSIES?

Day Five
July 5 – Stoke on Trent, Newcastle

Thom continued to be a gracious and helpful host the next morning. He took us to a supermarket where we ate breakfast at the cafe in front and then laid in a few provisions. I picked up water and many rolls of Trebor's mints – a British candy that I have a terrible weakness for. Seamus bought some zucchini. We dropped Thom off back at home and turned towards the north.

They wanted to get the oil changed in the van, so they pulled into a quick change business on the way out of Stoke. This was when Marco's tendency to refer to everyone else as a "retard" came into sharp focus. The man behind the counter helpfully explained that the size of the van meant that they couldn't do it at his location and that there weren't many other locations he knew of that were big enough to handle a large van like ours. Somehow when this got related to the band half an hour later he had turned into a retard who didn't know what he was talking about.

An hour later we were hurtling down the motorway towards Newcastle when, as had happened many times over the past couple of days, the rain started. As I mentioned previously, the windshield wipers didn't work. At all. Period. Not even worth trying.

"Driving is fine" explained Marco, "it's just that if someone fucks up I can't stop in time."

Translation: "As long as I don't have to stop or maneuver this massive vehicle moving at 120 kmph, we'll all be okay."

This was the heaviest rainfall we'd seen yet. Sitting in the middle of the van, all I could see out the front window was a psychedelic wash of splashes, waves, and streams. Remember, the rain wasn't just falling on the windshield – it was colliding with it at high speed. A pattern of grey and silver blotches that obliterated the view of whatever was in front of us. At one point Marco took his water bottle in hand, screamed "is that the best you can do, you pussies?" and splashed the inside of the windscreen to match the mess on the outside. Naturally I found myself thinking "I could die here."

I have a theory that the people who think that young people see themselves as immortal are missing the point. I don't think they believe that they can't die – I think that they don't have enough personal experience with death to appreciate how fucking awful the results of their actions can be. Or even death's only slightly less horrific brother "lying in a hospital bed, covered in scrapes, bruises, and scratches, with a variety of casts and bandages." There's no point of reference to measure the risk against.

Me? I've been around just enough to have some good friends die and feel the excruciating pain of a minor mishap (like a full scraping slide across pavement after my bicycle wheel jammed in a streetcar track), to know what it would do to the people I love if I were to take a dirt nap, especially in a really stupid way. I'm no expert on death or pain, but it doesn't take much experience with both of them to know that they both suck in the biggest possible way. So I sat in that seat and my thought process went something like this...

I could do one of three things here. I could either say "pull off the road and wait for the rain to stop you fucking moron before you get us all killed." Or I could calmly ask to be dropped off at the nearest town where I could catch a train and meet them, hopefully, at the next venue. Or I could just suck it up. In for a penny, in for a pound. I wanted the touring experience, and by god I was getting it.

This Place Is Awesome

I'd been able to separate myself from most of the idiocy so far, if only in my own mind. I could listen to the endless, base, crude humour and not join in – I could observe and follow along without feeling like I was enabling or contributing to it. But here I had to bite down hard and either be a party to the stupidity or forever make it clear that I was not really a team player. I wouldn't really be "on tour," just "with the tour." I thought about the recent horror of another Vancouver band who flipped their van on the Trans-Canada Highway and lost their much-loved drummer. I thought of how my wife would react when I told her this story.

After weighing the pros and cons, considering the options, and checking the contents of my shorts (clean and dry), I decided to keep my mouth shut and ride the crazy train all the way through stupidville.

Of course we didn't die. I have to assume that it was a combination of careful concentration on the vague patterns that he could make out in the chaos and a lot of shit luck. Not only did we not hit anything, but I can't say we even had to brake in a noticeable way. I'm not in a hurry to do that again though – I don't like to poke fate in the eye like that.

On the way to Newcastle, with that unsettled feeling of being unsure of my place that first appeared in Chepstow casting an increasingly dark shadow, I started to sense a grim view of the situation taking over.

It's a low grade Lord of the Flies situation. These five young men, set adrift from the filters that normally keep their behaviour in check, may not be dressing in animal skins and putting hog's heads on spikes, but their civility and maturity have taken a hit. When people asked me how it was to be on tour with The Dreadnoughts, my answer was "interesting" – interesting in that way that a painting is "interesting." Interesting here is a stand in for "I'm not sure what to make of it." It had fun moments, without a doubt, and over time those are the things that stand out and get remembered, but I would hesitate to call it "fun." There was humour and camaraderie and moments that brought us all closer together. But as I read through the notes I took at the time, I'm reminded of how difficult it was. How basic courtesy fell away to a low-grade selfishness.

It's important to put this in context. These are not just a bunch of young beer-drinking yahoos. There is a surprising level of intelligence in this van. One of the band members is a teaching assistant in the philosophy department at a major university. Another teaches physics at a university level. One of the others walked away from a mathematics scholarship. I found myself trying to understand why this bunch of ambitious, bright, young men, doing the thing they loved to do, involved in the kind of an international adventure that many people dream of, would treat each other like crap.

They were not malicious – no one was actively trying to sabotage or demean anyone else. But there was very little courtesy. None of them would ask the others how they were doing. No one held the door open for the next person – literally or figuratively. They simply took what they needed to keep from going crazy and let everyone else sort themselves out. So while they didn't actively try to cut each other out or make one another miserable, it was also notable that they wouldn't offer up a seat or any of their time in the interest of making someone else's life more bearable. It took me a long time to understand why they would behave like this. Why anyone would behave like this?

What I came to realise was that it was a matter of limited resources. The life they were leading was one where there was very little comfort to take – limited food, limited money, fewer beds than bodies, few people to talk intelligently to, and especially little privacy. When something came up you didn't look at it and decide who needed it most, or how to split it equitably – you simply grabbed what you needed and didn't look around to see what effect it had. The reason it worked is that there are no real prima donnas in this band. No one seemed to think that they deserved considerably more than anyone else, and there was an innate sense of how much one could reasonably take. It wasn't unusually tense around the boys, although there was certainly a degree of complaining about each other. They just seemed to have found a manageable and consistent level of universal disgruntledness. To an outside observer it all seemed a bit sad and exhausting. I now believe it was just their way of pacing themselves.

When bands split up - especially bands that have a good following - there is usually a sense of confusion and disbelief amongst the fans. Any decent live band will have the appearance of being a family on stage - all pulling together, playing their individual parts towards a common goal. Great bands will make it look like they couldn't possibly want to be anywhere else, with any other people in the world. It's seldom recognised that many bands aren't shining examples of cooperation and mutual respect, they are unlikely collections of people who almost coincidentally play the same songs. It's like they are all on the same bus. They just happened to be going in the same direction, so they agree to travel together. Rarely, if ever, does it have anything to do with understanding each other's personal needs and wanting to share and help in their human and artistic potential.

The Dreadnoughts were all good friends. They spent time together, drinking and socializing, at home in Vancouver, outside of the time they were acting as a band. It was part of the unspoken purpose of the band that it allow them to hang out with each other. But most friends don't live with each. They don't spend weeks crammed into a speeding van together. That would stretch the capacity of any friendship. Hell, it pushes some marriages beyond the brink. The question one has to ask, if one is really that curious, is not "why would friends like that treat each other poorly?", it's "why would friends put their perfectly decent friendship to such a test?" The answer is somewhere at the intersection of youthful bravado, social and intellectual curiosity, artistic drive, and the lure of getting drunk for free on previously unknown types of liquor.

Humour in the tour van was generally a dark thing. It's frequently mean-spirited, sexist, obsessed with sex, body parts, and scatology, unsophisticated, and centred around put downs. It is to humour what strip clubs are to entertainment – on the surface it's supposed to entertain, but it's really just kind of sad, lonely, and laced with desperation. It's only by mutual assent that it's considered funny and acceptable. To be fair, these boys were no more prone to or enthusiastic about it than any other group of young men. It's a universal bonding ritual. I guess the problem I had was that I couldn't escape it. Normally I either challenge it or walk away – neither was going to be appropriate in this situation.

Given the level of intelligence that was on this tour, I was a bit surprised at how much time was spent keeping that intelligence under wraps. Vast stretches of time were spent in bored silence, fratboy humour, or various stages of inebriated shouting. In hindsight I can pick out moments when they engaged in something other than playing, drinking, or waiting for something to happen – The Apple, St Paul's Carnival, Wilkins Cider Farm, Chepstow Castle, The Baltic Flour Mill – and it would be easy to have the amount of time spent just sitting around waiting for something to happen slip from my memory. But I have too many scribbled notes that riff on the theme "bored bored bored bored." I commented earlier on how the band rarely seized the opportunity to actively explore. I realise this might be my own personal bias creeping in. Maybe they were doing what most tourists do. Or maybe it was just that point in the tour for them. They'd spent a month in countries where they didn't speak the language, trying to muddle through and being overwhelmed by the strangeness of it all. Here in Britain they could let their guard down and just exist without much effort. I'll happily cut them some slack and not make any assumptions. But the undeniable truth of the matter is that there was an awful lot of staring blankly into space, combined with curling up on any flat surface and trying to catch a few minutes of sleep.

And so it was in this environment of sitting and waiting, punctuated by moments of vaguely desperate humour, being slowly eaten away by lack of decent sleep, and increasingly unsure of what I was doing there or whether I was wanted, that I started to crack. In hindsight I think it was proof that I was, indeed, a part of the action and not just an observer. I had reached the same state as the rest of them – just perhaps a little quicker. I had even found myself starting to participate in the crude humour and general edginess. It was a potent force and it became hard not get swept up in the landslide towards the lowest ground. The effort required to fight back was intense and usually had no effect, which ended up giving it more fuel. As I gave up what humanity I had, the disappointment in myself became the fuel for my own contributions. To call it self-loathing would be going much too far. But it can't be denied that a lot of the jokes had that whiff of trying to make oneself feel better by degrading others.

Having been in "around the clock" observation mode at this traveling asylum – trying to catch, examine, and dissect every action and behaviour, both theirs and mine – I was in need of a rest.

There was a show that night in Newcastle and then a day off. General consensus was that we would probably spend the day in Newcastle, everyone going their own way. Not a moment too soon.

The band loaded into the venue in the same way they had done a hundred times on this tour alone. A slow, routine, schlepping of the same time, tired, beer-soaked equipment, down yet another steep staircase, into yet another dark room, and up onto yet another modest stage of plywood and black paint.

Probably the most unreliable part of the whole process was the soundperson. It seems every small club in the world has a soundperson who arrives on their own, unique schedule. Sometimes they are there waiting for you when you arrive; other times you sit around and get increasingly anxious until they blow in with ten minutes to spare and insist that there's no need for anything more than a line check (which is a process by which you hit each instrument in turn and as long as some kind of noise comes out of the speaker then you are good to go). They can be more unpredictable - in their sense of timing, degree of interest, and level of appreciation - than the crowds. Some bands seem to take an instantly adversarial relationship with most soundpeople, which seems foolish given that the band are putting their professional lives in the hands of this person who has the power to weaken the performance to the point of disaster. I've always tried to make a special effort to be friendly and helpful to soundpeople; it's a tiring, difficult, and frequently thankless job. I've never regretted being nice to one. (Lighting operators, on the other hand, often seem to land their job as some form of charity or a work placement plan for hopelessly unskilled people with poor eyesight, lousy hearing, and a profoundly overinflated sense of self-worth. A good lighting tech is a rare and invaluable treat to someone like me.) The Dreadnoughts are generally pretty oblivious to the soundperson, and in Newcastle he matched the band's weary, indifferent approach to the soundcheck making the process perfunctory but satisfactory. With that out of the way, it was time to find something to eat.

One of the things that bothers me the most about visiting new places is the capacity for wasting time with details that any local could deal with in a fraction of the time. Finding food is a prime example. On this occasion, for reasons I can't remember, the meal was not provided by the venue so we had to go find food ourselves.

It's easy in these situations to fall back on familiar but god-awful options. Subway, McDonalds, KFC - no matter what obscure corner of the world you find yourself in, you could easily spend an entire tour eating in places like those because they are uncomfortably ubiquitous, instantly recognisable, and you know that whatever you buy is going to be the same thing you were capable of stuffing in your face back home. It's the most efficient way to find food, but it's also the most efficient way to find yourself pale, sick, fat, and stupid by the end of a tour. It's also an almost criminal act to travel the world and sample nothing but the local rendition of the universal Quarter Pounder recipe.

Given the band's unwillingness to sink to those depths, the alternative was to head out into the streets and see what they could find. We did the only sensible thing first and asked a local which direction we should head if we wanted to find something to eat. They directed us to a busy street a couple of blocks from the venue that sloped down to the river and was lined with shops and restaurants.

On the way out, Nick stopped in a small side street to negotiate with a homeless guy who had offered to sell him a guitar. Moments later he caught up to us, triumphantly holding up his new purchase - a guitar that appeared to be in need of only a small repair to the nut (the piece at the top of the fretboard where the strings are held in place).

The spot recommended to us as a place with good restaurants was, indeed, a great place to go for a nice meal. Sadly it failed in three important respects - the restaurants were expensive, they were places to sit down and spend the evening (we had only an hour or so), and they were not likely to be too pleased with our appearance.

The day to day uniform of the band was utilitarian, dingy, and either in need of repair or covered in patches. It was clothing for comfort and convenience, not fashion. In a way, of course, this is its own fashion statement. But it was a statement that said, amongst other things, "we are no more interested in being around affluent, well-dressed people having a quiet, expensive meal, than you are interested in having us at the table next to you." It was street urchin clothing. I had carefully packed seven changes of clothes for the seven days I would be with the band. They had no such luxury.

So we kept walking down the street, hoping to find something more suitable. The frustrating part of this that I alluded to earlier is the knowledge that the street you might be looking for - full of great, cheap food - might be one block over from the street you are on. There's not really any way of knowing if you're two blocks or two kilometers from just what you're after.

In the end, fate gave us a break in the form of a little donair shop. We tucked into some simple, hearty, and cheap food and walked back to the venue.

The show went off well. A new twist was added to The Tower of Power. While Seamus was on top of Andrew's shoulders singing, he was simultaneously pouring wine into Andrew's mouth. The Newcastle crowd were a bit standoffish. Or more accurately, "stand-off-in-the-back-of-the-room-ish." Unlike the Eastern European crowds who had embraced the band from the first note and established themselves as energetic and keen, the British audiences would often seem interested but reserved. I noticed the Newcastle audience chanting along as instructed, but doing it from a position where they could lean up against the bar, as opposed to at the front of the stage. I even saw people dancing in their chairs. Not on their chairs, but in their chairs. Some force was keeping them from showing too much enthusiasm.

I want to take a moment to talk about Drew. It's going to be a very brief moment, because there's not a lot to say. Drew doesn't give up much. He doesn't appear in many of these stories (or at least he doesn't appear by name) because he is easily the quietest and most withdrawn one. There is also a darkness to Drew that is instantly recognisable. Where I have dreadlocks because I thought it would be fun and a strange kind of ode to some musical heroes, Drew wears his in a way that seems to be intended to make it very clear that he wants to be on the outside – same goes for the numerous and conspicuous body piercings. He is appropriately friendly when approached, but any deeper connection with him is going to be on his terms and his turf. I don't profess for a moment to know what makes him tick.

Drew as a character in this story is most memorable to me for his performances during The Skrigjaargen Polka.

Typically The Dreadnoughts' songs run at a pretty good clip. On this tour it seemed like they were trying to beat some kind of speed record. Certain songs started out fast and just became a blur by the end. The Skrigjaargen Polka was a prime example.

I was surprised to see this song on the Victory Square CD when it got released – I was at the recording sessions and I didn't remember the song being mentioned. It turns out that this is the final name of what used to be referred to as "Mando Commando," because it features Drew's mandolin playing. And for those of you who are curious, "Skrigjaargen" is a made up word. Now put down the atlas and pay attention.

Mando Commando starts out slowly and builds, both in volume and in speed. By the end of the song Drew and Seamus are frequently lying in a sweaty, exhausted heap on the stage, unable to divert any of their attention to anything but their hands to keep the pace. This song has also done a lot to bring Drew out of his shell and give him a chance to shine. Drew is an excellent mandolin player, and a man with a prodigious knowledge of folk music. Drew's mandolin is, sonically, perhaps the equivalent of a rhythm guitar, and in terms of stage presence Drew tends to be a reliable but comparatively low key player. He sings and pumps his fist in the air when he's not playing, but next to characters like Nick, Seamus, and Andrew he comes across as the quiet one. During Mando Commando he takes centre stage and he dominates it. Off stage, Drew would occasionally bark out an amusing comment but mostly he just kept to himself.

After the Newcastle show, excited by the prospect of an afterhours event named "Get Your Skates On" (which I initially heard as "Get Your Skirt On" – the Newcastle accent is notorious), the band followed our local hosts to what was supposed to be a late night of ska music and free drinks. In the end it was a pretty standard university dance pub/pool hall and the free drinks never really materialised. Nevertheless we socialised and played pool for a few hours. The band had accepted my cousin's offer of a place to stay but by the end of the night, after a frustrating hour of trying to round up the boys, it was just Nick and I that were heading out. The rest of them had found locals who were offering places to stay, and presumably were as eager for some time away as I was.

Durham was meant to be a 20 minute drive by van. I seized the opportunity to climb behind the wheel, being the only one sober and knowing that the streets would be largely deserted at that hour of the night. It probably took us at least an hour to get there, in no small part due to my cousin's peculiar tendency to freeze up at critical moments when giving directions ("Go left here. No. Wait. Go Right. Oh damn, it was left after all. Sorry.")

I won't describe the state of his flat because I'm saving that information up for when I need to blackmail him. Let's just say it was, in most respects, in keeping with the standard to which I was becoming accustomed. I curled up on the couch, looking forward to a day off the next day. Sleep came quickly. Sadly, so too did the dawn.

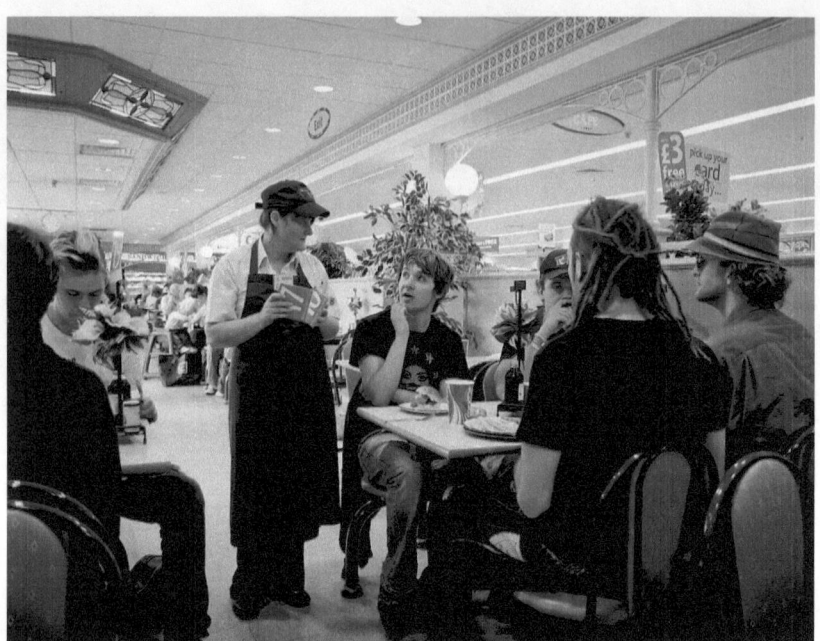

Pure class - breakfast at the local supermarket.

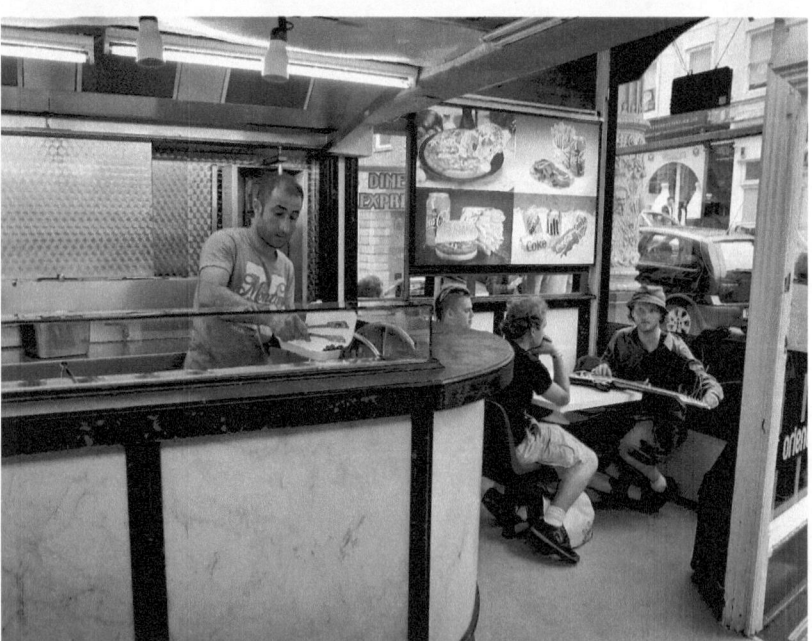

Dinner at a donair shop in Newcastle.

This Place Is Awesome

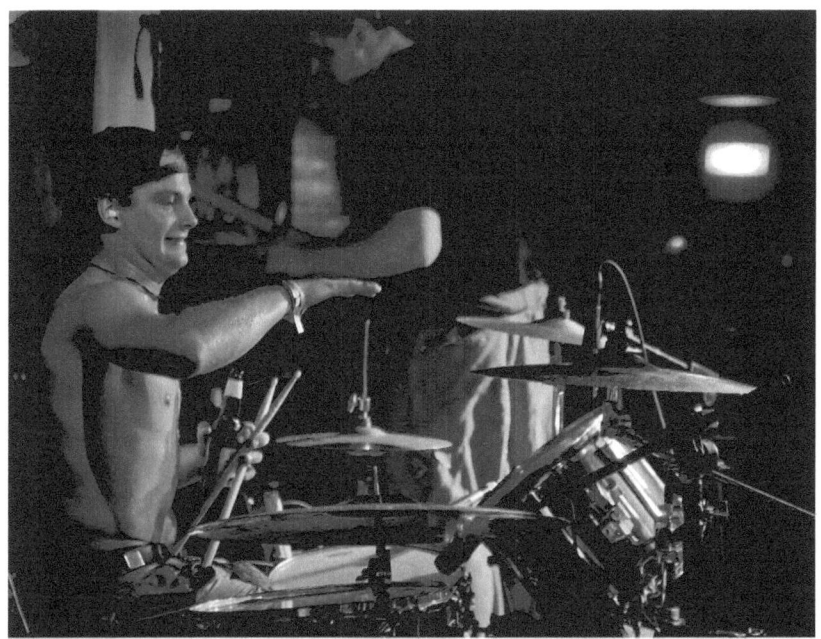

Marco – beer and drumsticks in his left hand while he checks how steady he is with this right hand.

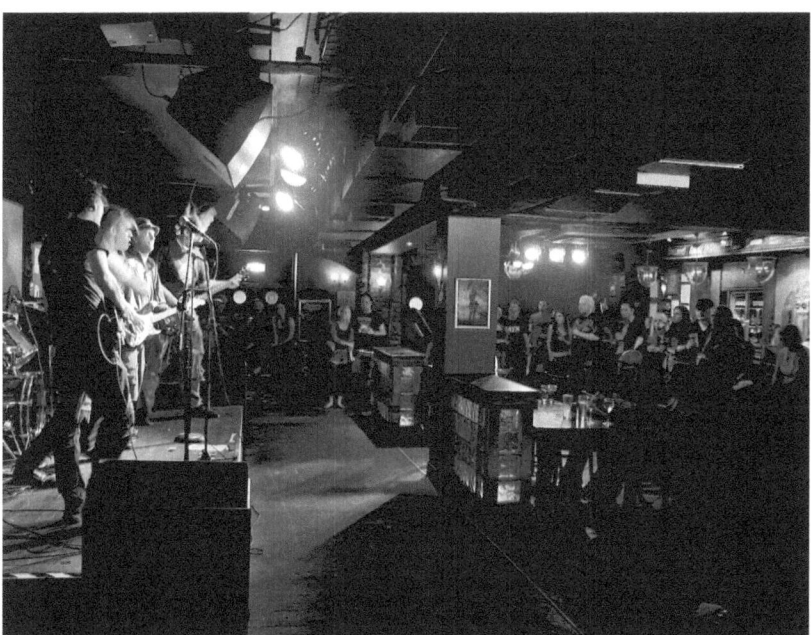

The Newcastle crowd is appreciative and energetic, but they will not be moved from their seats. Some of them are dancing and shouting – from their seats...

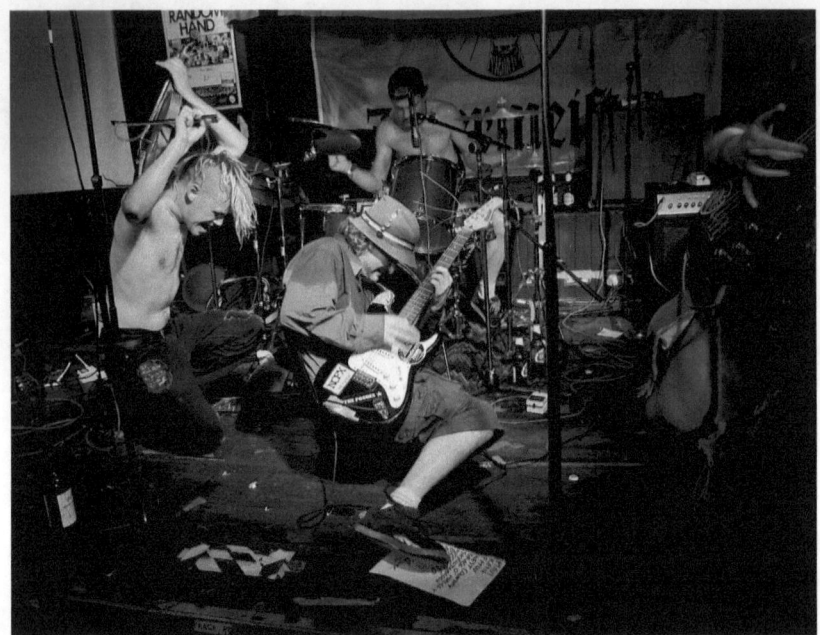

... but it was not from lack of effort on the stage.

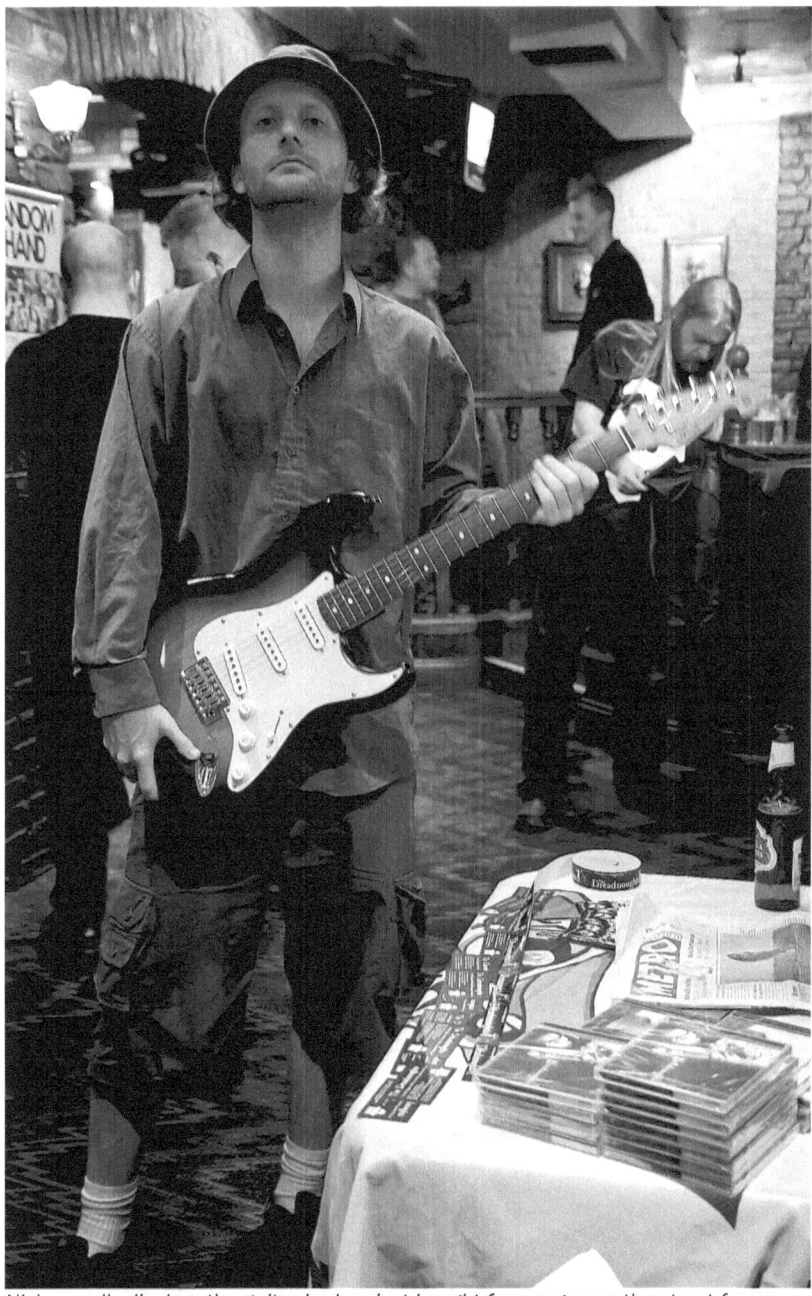

Nick proudly displays the guitar he has just bought from a guy on the street for an absurdly small amount of money.

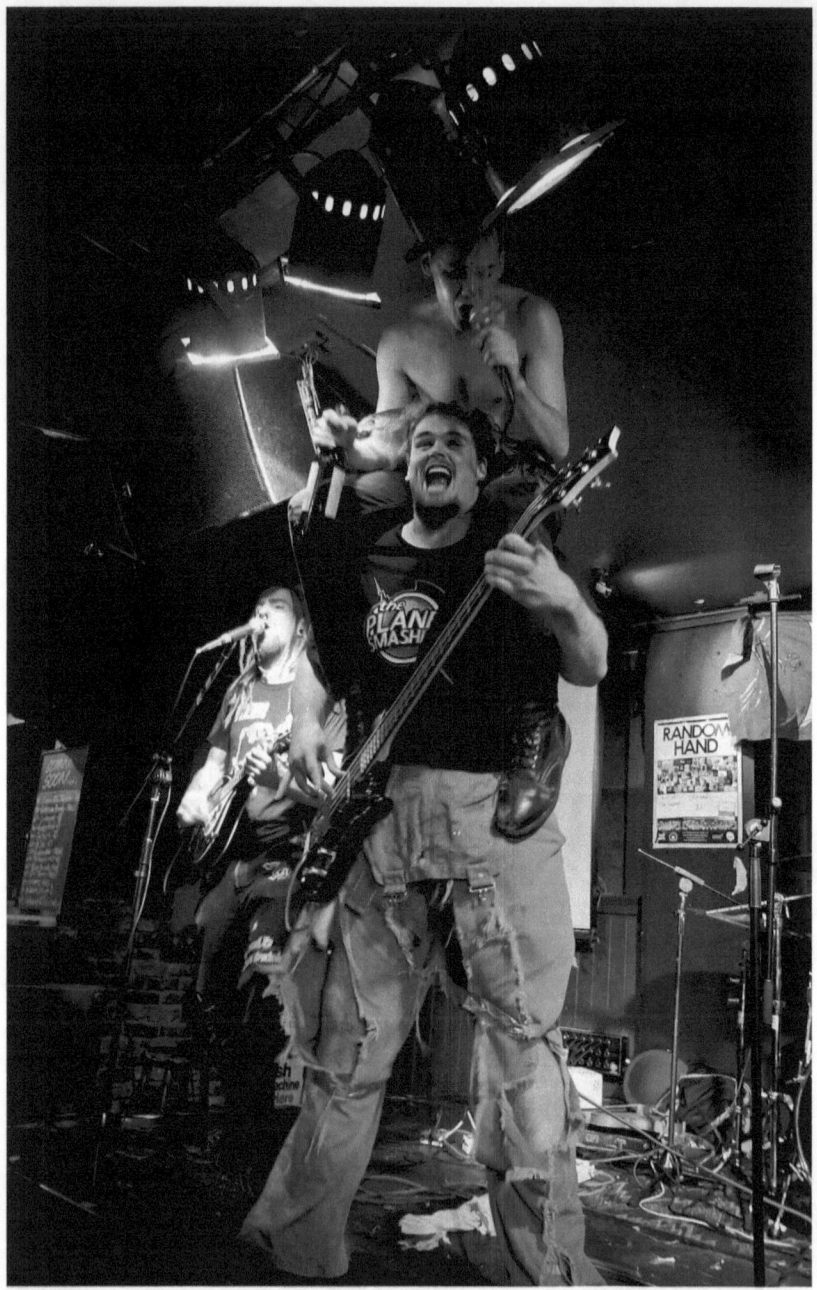

The legendary "Tower of Power." Just before Seamus poured half that bottle of wine down Andrew's throat.

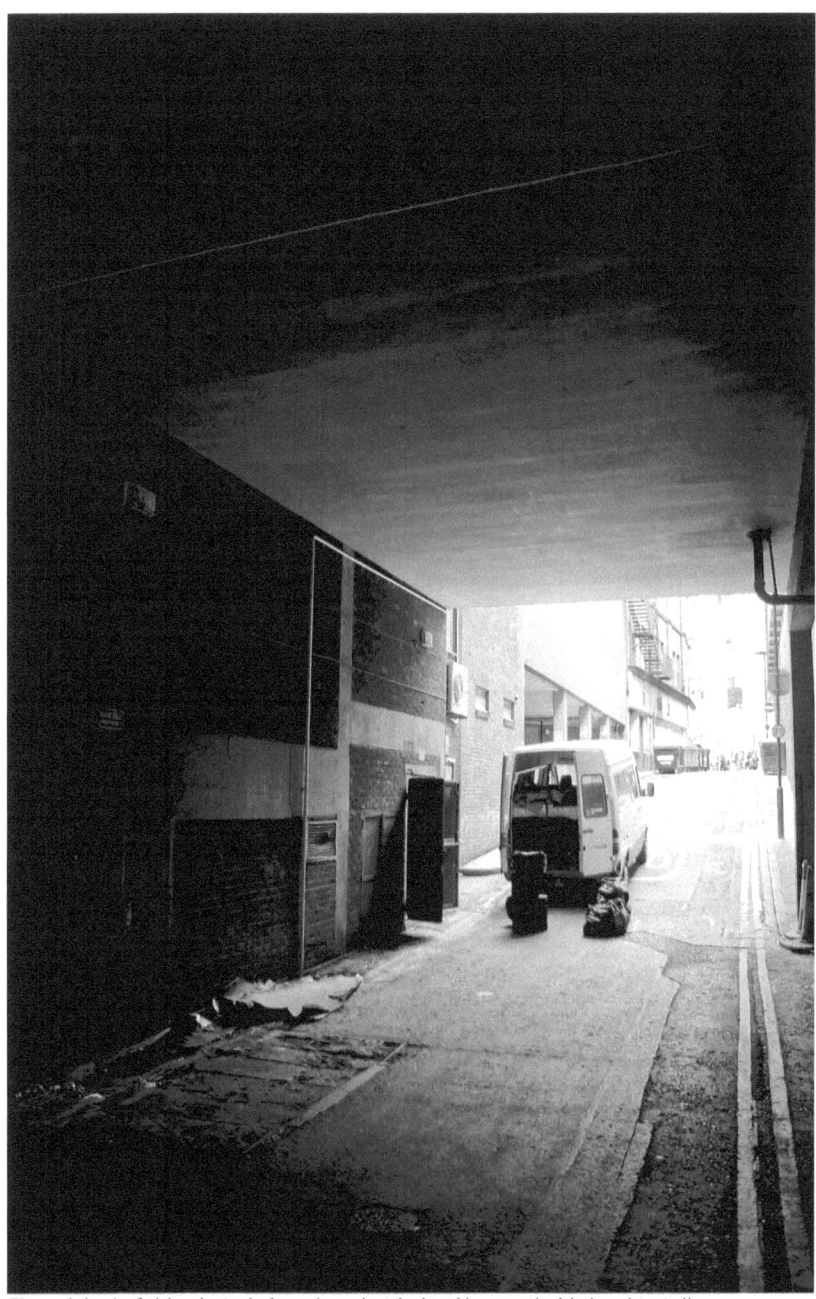

The original of this photo is in colour, but being Newcastle it's hard to tell.

This Place Is Awesome

IF YOU
COULD GO
HOME NOW,
WOULD YOU?

Day Six
July 6 – Newcastle

I was woken by my alarm reminding me that I needed to plug the parking meter. I then had another cold shower experience. This time there was a new element to the horrific exploit. The peculiar box that was installed inside the shower, which I am told is the water heater, had strange markings around the controls. You know the movie Total Recall? Well I was reminded of the alien technology in that film. I couldn't figure out if I was meant to press the button next to the symbol that looked like Che Guavara getting a manicure, or turn the knob next to the symbol of the art deco ashtray falling into a vat of frowning jello. I didn't get any hot water out of the system, but I may have launched an alien invasion at some point.

Nick and I climbed back into the van and, without the dubious benefit of a local navigator, we made it back to the venue without a single wrong turn. A moderately coherent band vote resulted in a decision to spend most of the day in town and drive on to Peterborough in the late afternoon. Seamus's vote came in via text message from an unfamiliar number. He'd found a local to spend some time with.

Seamus is a sweetheart in every sense. Of the whole emotionally stunted bunch, he's the most likely to be watching out for other people's comfort. I'd seen this clearly demonstrated at home in Vancouver, and even here in the din and despair of the tour it came out in little pieces. He's also the heartthrob of the band – if you are the kind of person who goes for the drunken punk, railroad hobo look. He quietly seeks out affection and attention, and easily makes a connection with the young locals. They typically strike me as attractive young women with low grade self-esteem issues – the kind who would be easy prey for musicians with high-grade self-esteem problems and little conscience. He knows how it looks and he is quick to defend his, and their, honour. I believe him whenever he insists the relationships are platonic.

Nick and I returned to street level to look around a little. It was the first chance I'd had for some proper time to hang out with Nick when we weren't both exhausted at the end of a long day. In hindsight I realised that Nick and I had spent a lot of time together, although it wasn't until this day I finally got to speak to him like a human being. You know - the kind that isn't on tour with a young punk band. While he'd probably be the last to admit it, I suspect he was gravitating towards me because I was the only one trying desperately to maintain some higher level of function and intelligence. I was happy to spend time around Nick for the same reason. The rest of them had simply surrendered to the howling dumbs. The pressure to tow the party line was very strong, and I while do enjoy acting like a goof for a while I also need to reassert my civility from time to time.

He's a thoughtful guy – both professionally as a philosophy student and teaching assistant, and just generally - but I've never been particularly successful at scraping off the crustiness and getting past the awkward provocateur act. Which is a shame, because any moron can yell insults at a crowd but few people can really make you think. I often try to get Nick to let the thoughtful side out for a walk but I suspect that he needs to be the curmudgeonly lush to prove to himself that he's not becoming an elitist intellectual prat. I have this sense that somewhere in Vancouver is a collection of people that only know the other Nick, and would be equally surprised to see his "Uncle Touchy" persona.

Walking down the street I asked him "If someone offered you half of all your guarantees from the rest of the tour and said you could just go home now, would you?" If I'd asked him a couple of days earlier he would have seriously considered it. On that day he was feeling better about things. It really is a day to day existence. No one was thinking about Peterborough that day. That was tomorrow. It would get there soon enough.

We walked down the main street downtown and I felt relaxed for the first time in what seemed like ages. There was no pressure, no annoying chatter, no requirements – we had some time to close our mouths, open our eyes, and look around for a change. We visited the column commemorating Lord Earl Grey, who was evidently not only a tea drinker of note, but also a defender of many decent virtues, including peace and civility. We gave him his due and thanks and moved on. There are no statues in Canada (that I've seen) to commemorate people who made great social improvements. We do well with the medical heros, but we could do with a couple of social justice heros.

I took Nick to his first Waterstones. Waterstones is a chain of British bookstores, which may not seem like a big deal. We have big bookstores in Canada. Chapters is similar in market penetration. But where Chapters continues to shout about how wonderful they are while quietly removing books to make room for scented candles and throw pillows, Waterstones is very clearly about books. Good books. Yes, they have their shite, but I can't walk out of a Waterstones without three books (they always seem to have a "three for two" sale going on). They're not even my favourite British bookstore, but I still love them. Not a huge surprise for a country that has such a reputation for valuing literacy and erudition. The English are great with words. The rest of the world may kick their asses at all the sports that they invented, and the things they do to vegetables in the name of meal preparation can be criminal, but they are the undisputed champions of the English language as far as I'm concerned.

Nick was on a mission to find a "real" pub and we'd been told we should head down to the water – the River Tyne in this case. At the foot of a long hill of shops we found a row of three pubs. We settled on the first one because it looked appropriately dark, woody, and authentic. They had a "two meals for 5.95 UKP" deal, so I abandoned my resolve to eat a salad and decided on steak and ale pie. Nick ordered bangers and mash. No... seriously. Bangers and mash. The food took a long time to come but when it did we were both in mouth-watering heaven. My meal tasted like it was really made there, not just delivered frozen and heated in a microwave. From the first bite I started to melt. I don't know why it hit me so hard, but it was one of the best meals I'd had in ages. Nick was similarly pleased.

I snapped a few pictures of Nick. The scene was perfect – light coming in from the window, dark rich wood background. He looked too happy for me to miss capturing the moment. He looked like a porcupine that had finally let all his quills settle down for a few minutes.

On the way back to the venue – where we had agreed to gather and then leave for Peterborough – we stopped at a cafe for a coffee and a moment of internet access. The female server asked where we were from and Nick replied "Vancouver." The waitress burst into a moment of energetic exclamations and high-fived Nick vigorously. I was caught off guard by the assertiveness, not to mention the enthusiasm. The British had not demonstrated much in the way of enthusiasm so far on this trip. It turned out that she had moved to Newcastle from Vancouver seven years ago. She had never run into anyone from Vancouver and was very pleased to find some hometown people in her newly adopted home. We settled into a couple of decent coffees and a moment of checking email.

Then it was back to the venue and the obligatory hour and a half of uncertainty about what to do next. Everyone was there, wandering in and out at random moments, except Seamus. Marco found his internet connection, so we knew he was going to be stationary and occupied for a while. Even when everyone was present and amenable to making a decision it could sometimes take a peculiar amount of time to achieve consensus. This was one of those times. I took a run to find some postcards. In WH Smith I discovered the absolutely classic British granny. I almost howled at how perfect she was – 4 foot 8, gran coat, little tam, hunched over. Straight out of a Giles cartoon.

I returned to the venue from my short jaunt for yet more waiting and hemming and hawing. The decision was finally made to stay in Newcastle another night and I resolved to take a proper break and splash out on a hotel room. I was feeling great about having at least one night where I could be in control of the basics - food, scheduling, accommodations. I offered Nick the second bed for whatever he was planning on paying for his youth hostel accommodations plan. He accepted. I had seen a Premier Inn down by the river next to the bridge and that seemed like the simplest approach. This particular bridge is famous for Kittywakes, a species of seagull that spends most of its life out at sea. The bridge is renowned for being the largest inland colony of these birds. It sounds like a nice idea. I later discovered that they are notorious amongst the locals for their prodigious ability to cover all surfaces in bird shit and make a relentless, ear-rattling racket.

Nick and I wandered down to the hotel and Nick waited outside while I checked in. I was carrying the baggage that would be normal for a traveller looking for a hotel room. Nick was disheveled, tired, dirty, and carrying a shopping bag. It just looked too much like an illicit sexual encounter for us to check in together. I mean I realise that no one there knew us and never will, and that it didn't matter what anyone else thought, but sometimes the line is internal and you just don't feel any need to cross it.

We drifted back to a small army surplus shop in search of a hat for Nick. He had earlier mentioned that he really wanted one. I pointed out that he was actually wearing a hat, but it turns out that it was Andrew's hat. To share or surrender it just wasn't on.

We walked up and down the river looking for another pub to drink in. Traipsing one way down the river lead to nothing decent, so we headed back the other way. A large building further down the other side turned out to be a museum of contemporary art and we made a move towards it. We walked across the Millennium bridge, which we discovered was actually the Millennium *Tilt* Bridge. It looked like a giant egg slicer at that moment and we were seriously unimpressed, but when we realised that it actually is tilted up every day to make a cool looking arch it took on a whole new level of awesome.

The gallery was the Baltic Gallery – named after the Baltic Flour Mill that was the original occupant of the building. There was a feature exhibit that purported to be interpretations of Darwin and selectionist theory.

It was the awful kind of modern art that is dangerously close to self-parody. One room had a giant, poor quality video of two Galapagos Island turtles mating. That was about as good as it got. When the most impressive and thought-provoking piece of art is indistinguishable from a funny YouTube video, I lose interest.

So we took the glass elevator up to the rooftop bar, had two triple gin martinis each, and sat looking out over the Tyne. We left the gallery, only slightly legless, and en route back to the tilt bridge we walked past the finish line of a fun run. A high school steel drum band was performing, which struck us both as a bit crap until Nick realised that they were playing Sweet Child Of Mine by Guns and Roses. Newcastle was full of surprises.

We made our way back to the Red House again – Nick's new favourite place – and settled into our customary booth by the window. Over the course of the next few hours we both got superbly drunk. We sent completely inappropriate text messages to Seamus who was still with the woman that he'd met at the venue. Nick was drinking many pints of Guinness and I packed away two gin and tonics and three pints of cider. I plugged up the jukebox with requests for Dave and Ansel Collins and Buddy Holly. It was either that or let the locals play Freebird for the tenth time.

The conversation flowed between serious and total nonsense until some time past midnight. It wasn't until a couple of months later, back in Vancouver, that the level of drunkenness we had achieved came back to haunt me. It turns out that we also took the time to write an obscene message on a postcard and mail it to Seamus's home address. I realise of course that we were doing exactly the thing that I have been so critical of until now – getting drunk and acting juvenile. All I can say in my defense is that I knew it was going to last for a few hours and then I'd be back to "normal." I leave it up to you to decide if I was being a hypocrite.

We staggered back to the hotel, which was mercifully across the street, and I had the long hot shower that I'd been dreaming about for days. Clearly the British hire foreign workers when it comes to installing plumbing in hotels. It was all blissfully familiar. I might have even got a decent night's sleep if it weren't for those fucking Kittywakes. I'm all for protecting wildlife, but would it really affect their species if we just tied their beaks shut between midnight and 0700h?

I had nearly cracked before that day. I might have been able to live like that 25 years ago, but I've had almost 15 years of living a civilised, comfortable life. I have nice stuff, I live amongst considerate, polite people, I eat well and I can depend on the people I know. This tour had been very, very different. The disorganisation, crudeness, irresponsibility, filth, and general low-key mayhem was extremely unpleasant, but these boys don't yet know what a really comfortable "grown up" lifestyle is

This Place Is Awesome

about, so it wasn't hard for them to take. Like I said – I could have done this when I was their age, and tolerated it fine. I can just about last a week at this point. Rock and roll at this level is a young person's game. It's hard to actually devolve yourself to this level after living for a while in your "dinner party" years. It's a lot easier as a young person to simply put your emerging development as an adult on hold for a bit. I couldn't guess as to whether they would willingly do that to themselves again. That tour in particular had too many dates and not enough breaks. For me, the day off had completely recharged me and I felt I could easily sail through two more days.

The truth is that it wouldn't actually take much to make a tour like that bearable – one day off a week and semi-regular decent accommodations would have made it so much easier to take. I sincerely hope that the seeds they were sowing on that tour will pay them back in basic creature comforts when they return. Things like the lack of cell phones was just dumb, but foregoing accommodations as a part of their requirements was completely understandable. It would have shot up the cost of the shows and they were eager to do the tour as cheaply as possible. They couldn't have possibly stayed out on the road that long, and played that many locations, if paying for hotels had been part of the deal. They may be reckless, but they are not stupid.

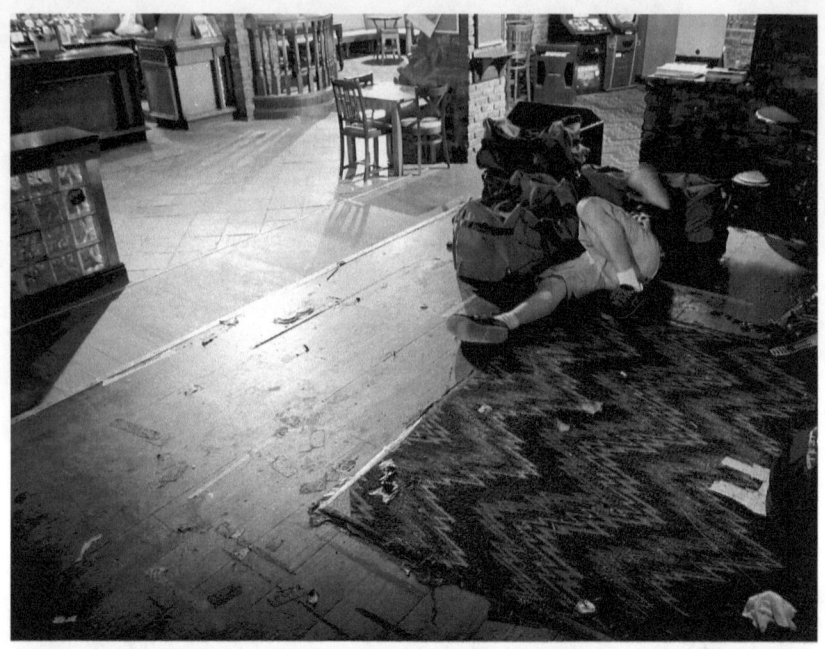

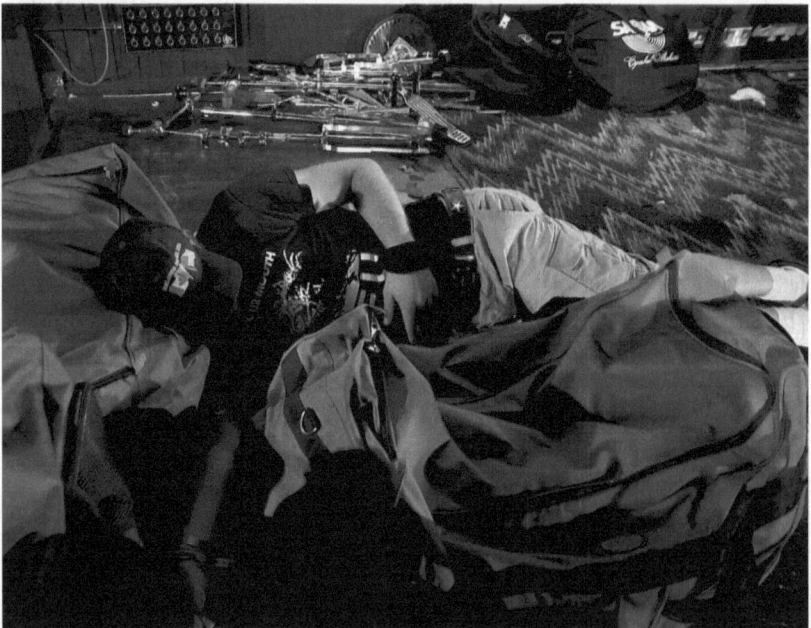

Marco slept in the club. It wasn't the worst sleeping conditions I'd seen.

This Place Is Awesome

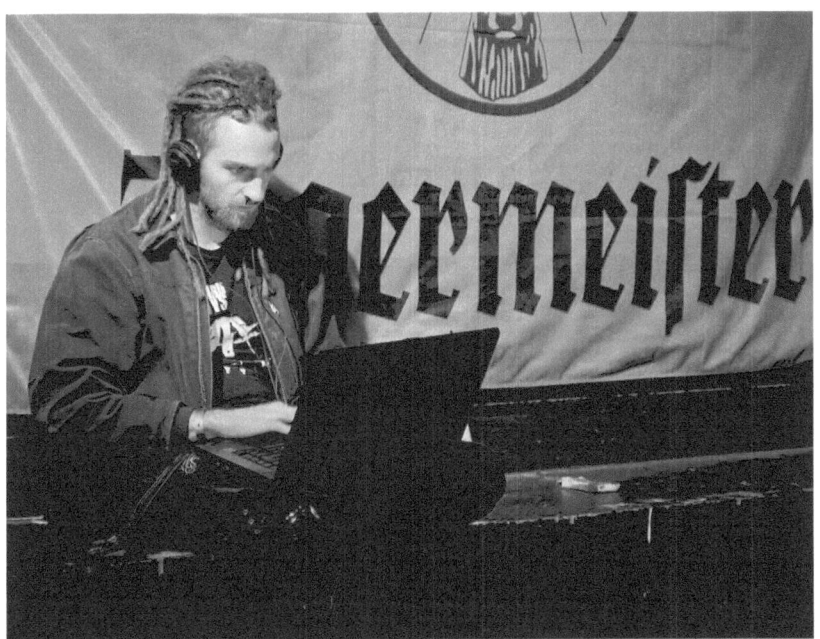
Drew takes his turn Skyping to friends back home.

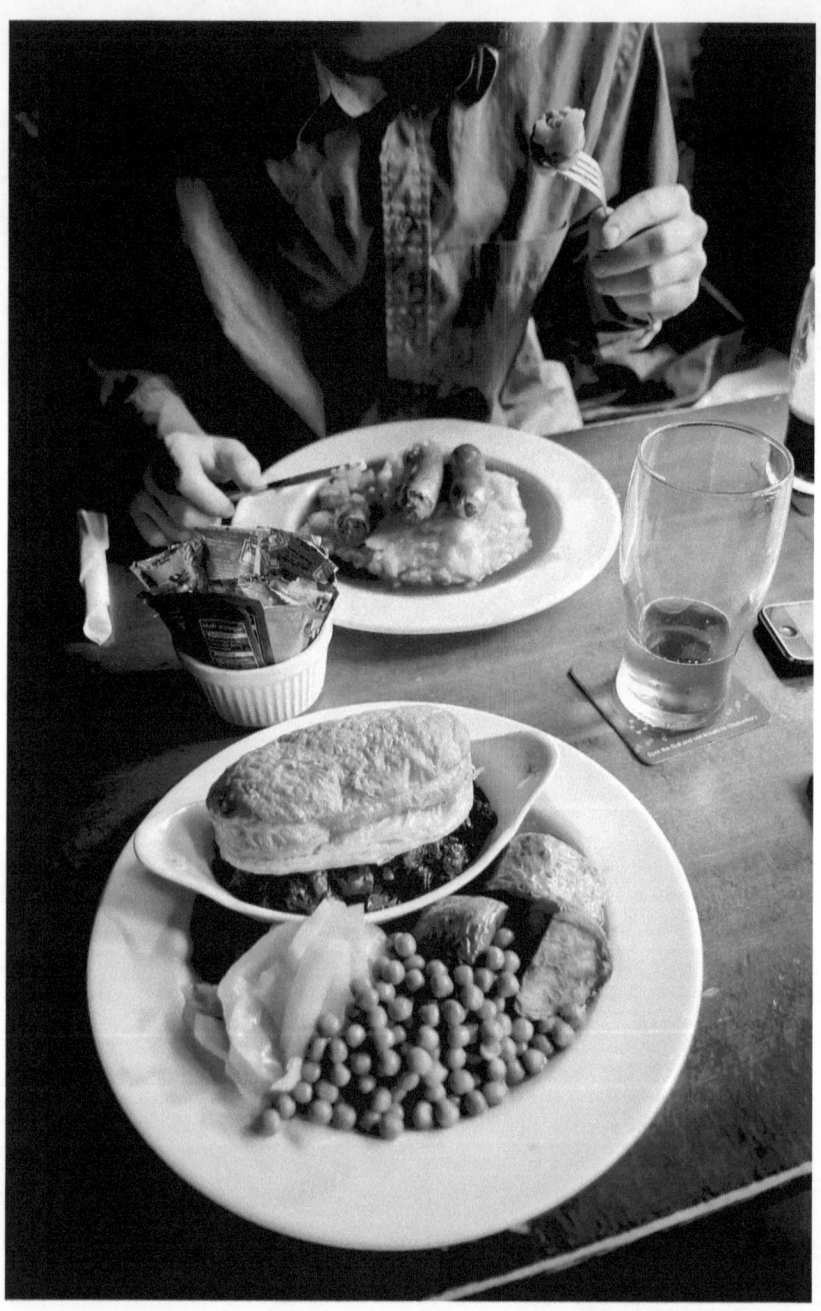

This Place Is Awesome

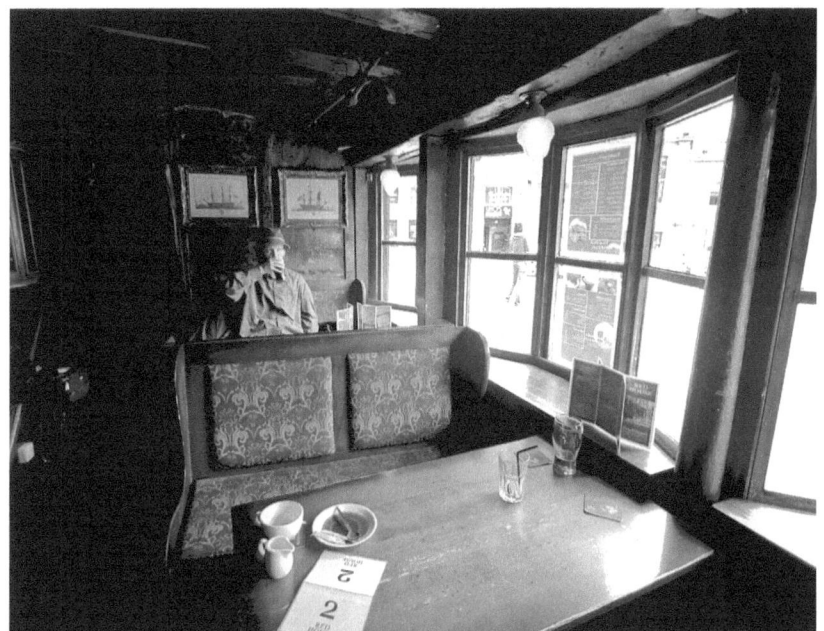

Nick finds comfort, calm, and the meal he's been seeking for days, in the Red House.

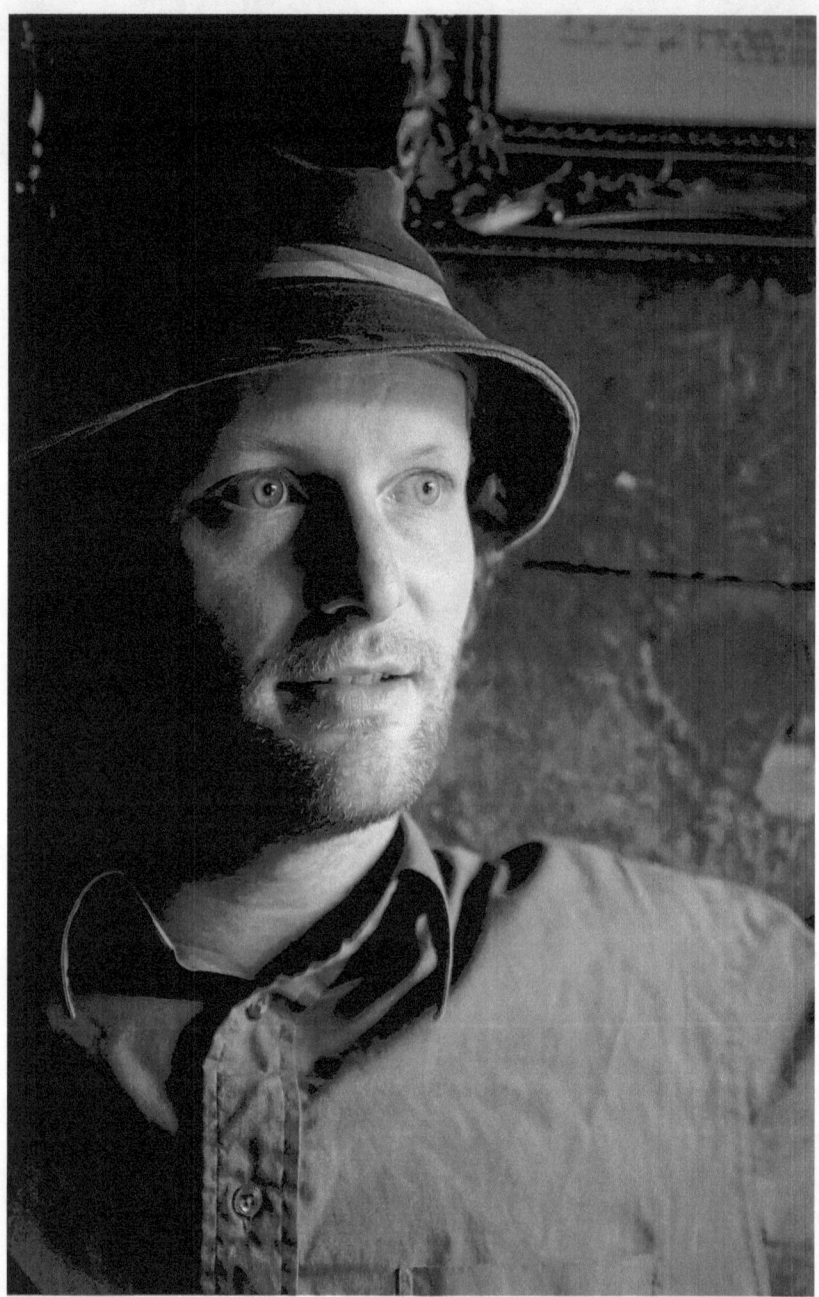

Nick, Newcastle.

This Place Is Awesome

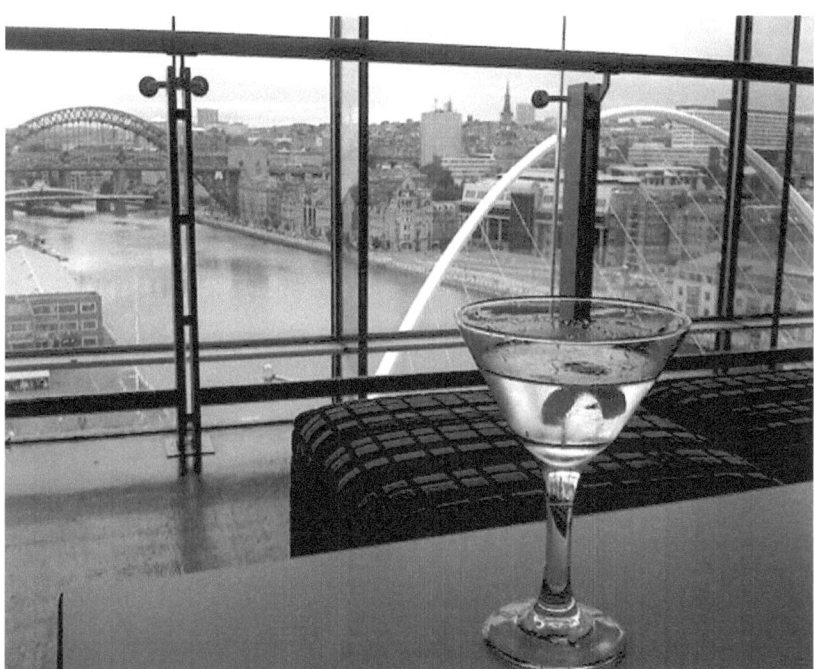

Tyne River Bridge, Millennium Tilt Bridge, lemon twist – an unintended study in arcs. A brief return to civility.

This Place Is Awesome

AM I BEING REWARDED OR PUNISHED?

Day Seven
July 7, 2009 - Newcastle, Peterborough

We all met at a library cafe across from the venue in the morning, climbed into the van, and set off towards the south. Leaving Newcastle we drove past The Angel of the North - a monolithic sculpture that looks like a single engine Cessna had got trapped in a giant clothes peg. That's just a cheap shot intended to get a quick laugh - it's actually quite an imposing and impressive piece of work.

Peterborough was the last full night I would spend on the road. It's a town north of London and the gig was a modest affair, but it left its mark on me in a couple of respects.

First of all the locals had some unusual local customs. At one point in The Dreadnoughts' set someone grabbed a stool from the bar along the wall and brought it into the middle of the floor. One audience member sat on the stool and then a bunch of others lifted the stool into the air and danced around. You've seen this before. You just haven't seen it at a gypsy punk gig – you've seen it at Jewish weddings. No one could explain to me why they did it.

Nor could they explain the pyramid. One young man raced to the front of the crowd, turned his back to the band, and held up his hands, making a triangle with his thumbs and forefingers. At that point, three young men fell on their hands and knees, followed by two guys who climbed onto their backs, followed by a final participant on top. Again... you've seen this behaviour before. But in this case it was in Frankie and Annette movies, or possibly your last pool party. I was impressed by the unity and unspoken sense of organisation required to do these slightly peculiar acts.

There were three local opening bands, the first one being a solo guitarist/singer with a social conscience. From the patio outside I made a crack that his pleading vocal line "I want freedom," which he repeated over and over again, sounded a bit like "I want Fritos." This led to a whole raft of snack related jokes.

With only two days left in Britain, the band needed to figure out how to get through the last gallon of West Country cider before they had to cross the border. England's drinking-in-public laws may be considerably more lax than Canada's, but much of the drinking had to be done at or around the venue, where it was bad form to bring your own alcohol. I said to Nick "Why don't you take it out of the big, conspicuous jug and pour it into water bottles? It looks like apple juice." Nick, Drew, and I engaged in a furious moment of inventive creativity, involving various water bottles, a pocket knife, and using the drinking cap from one bottle to safely transfer the precious liquid. Nick and Drew were delighted at the idea of being able to wander around happily swigging cider without offending anyone. Truth be told, so was I.

Peterborough was also the worst night of the tour for me in terms of accommodations. I'm still not sure if I was being rewarded or punished.

Most of the band were going to sleep in the van, having failed to secure any local couches or beds – largely due to the previously mentioned habit of not asking until all but three people had gone home. We were offered a place for two people to stay by one of the members of an opening band. It was decided that Andrew and I would go and everyone else would stay in the van. Right away that made me nervous. Andrew took up a huge amount of space and snored like a Cape Canaveral rocket launch. Was I being sent away with Andrew so that the rest of them could rest in comparative peace? They told me after the fact that they honestly thought they were giving up a comfortable night's sleep to me out of kindness. I have no doubt that they had no idea what the situation would really be like.

After a march through the empty streets of Peterborough – which was, in of itself, not an unpleasant thing on a quiet, late night – we arrived at the flat. The door opened on a scene that was quintessentially young, male, and probably single. The living room was awash in videogame cartridges, heavy metal music, empty beer cans, and, most distressing to me, overflowing ashtrays. I react badly to cigarette smoke – my eyes burn and I can start the countdown to the sniffling and cold symptoms. Also taking up space in the room in which we were meant to be sleeping were five, wide-awake young men who were quite content to keep playing videogames, playing music, and drinking. This is the kind of "partying" that many people falsely assume is highly desirable to a group of people who have just spent hours travelling, setting up, and playing a loud and energetic set of music (and have to start the whole process again in four hours time). I didn't want to be rude... well... I didn't want to be obviously rude but I was quite happy to get the point across that if I was being offered a place to sleep for the night, then I'd really be most interested in getting down to it. The most entertaining and generous thing they could have done for me and Andrew was turn off the lights and quietly slip upstairs.

But they were clearly not professional hosts, and so they kept the party going for a few more hours. Partly out of a desire for a passive aggressive form of protest, and partly to keep from having to breathe in a lot of second hand smoke, I bundled myself up in all my clothes, walked into the cool back garden, found a chair, and propped myself up against the cold brick wall in a vain attempt at getting some small bits of sleep.

Various characters wandered in and out of the back garden to smoke, leaving me wondering what on earth made them want to smoke outside when the entire living room was clearly a perfectly functional ashtray. Then I was joined by a sweet, waifish young woman with deep set eyes and a seemingly endless source of hand-rolled cigarettes that passed in a continuous stream from pocket to hand to mouth. She looked a little like the cartoon Emily The Strange, but with more of a heroin-chic skinniness. She professed to being painfully shy, as well as telling me how she's crap at geography at school, has never travelled further than Liverpool, is afraid to fly, loves hockey, and believes that the history she was taught in school is all state-sanctioned propaganda, implying either conspiracy or indoctrination – I was unclear on which and didn't care to pursue the matter. I tried to engage her in conversation, but at times my exhaustion got the better of me and all I could muster was a faint smile and nod. She wanted someone to talk to and was probably hoping that this load of strangers living the exotic rock and roll lifestyle would relate to her in a way that the locals can't. It's the kind of situation where a self-loathing, detached, callous young musician could easily take some advantage. Me – I was too married, too tired, too old, and too decent to even consider it. I appreciated the attention, but all I really wanted was for her go away without feeling slighted so that I could sleep.

Finally, at some point in the early hours, too late for me to remember, the party ran its course and I was able to clear a space between the cigarette butts on the floor to lie down.

I'm sure it seems perverse to the boys in the band, but I was actually a little disappointed that I never got to sleep in the van. I got the impression that it was the one indignity that, for some reason, I was intentionally spared. I can only imagine how uncomfortable, noisy, smelly, and generally non-conducive to sleep, or even rest, it must have been. But it was an unavoidable and consistent part of what they were experiencing. Perhaps they knew something I didn't. That one night spent trying to sleep in a van with that collection of drunken reprobates would have critically damaged any respect I had for them. Perhaps it was utterly selfish of them – "for god's sake, under no circumstances, let him sleep in the van. We need him."

Peterborough was also the beginning of the end for "the gig shirt."

This was Andrew's favourite shirt for performing in. Actually, it was the ONLY shirt he would perform in. Night after night. Long before I caught up with the boys in Bristol it had started to turn acrid. I simply don't have the vocabulary required to describe the state of this shirt (and that's saying something). Andrew never washed the gig shirt, he would just hang it off the back of the van to dry. Imagine soaking a towel in cat pee, wrapping it around your head, and walking into a vinegar fermenting tank. No... wait... not cat pee... make that wolverine pee, which I can only assume is just as vulgar but has a bit more muskiness to it. Seriously, it was the kind of thing that left you asking "can't I just stick my head up a skunk's ass instead?"

No one could explain to me why he was so attached to it. But I do know that the beginning of the end of the gig shirt was Peterborough and I'm prepared to tell you what else I know about it.

It wasn't a special shirt, as far as shirts go. It was just a regular thermal undershirt. And therein, of course, lies the first question. Why would anyone choose a shirt intended to keep you warm as an appropriate choice for climbing onto a hot stage and jumping around?

It had the words "Huge Styles" scrawled across it with magic marker. Again, I can't tell you why. It just became one of Andrew's self-assigned nicknames.

I was approached by the rest of the band in Peterborough and asked, in hushed, conspiratorial tones and out of earshot, if I would do the band a favour. "Of course I'll do you a favour. What do you need?" I asked, assuming they wanted me to watch the gear for a minute, or quietly slip some bottles into my camera bag.

"We need you to burn that shirt."

"Literally or figuratively?" I asked.

"Either way, it doesn't matter."

Evidently he had been confronted about the shirt in the past, but to no avail. Given the band's tendency to avoid approaching these sorts of things head on, I can imagine that the request wasn't delivered with the force and clarity that it warranted. I felt uncomfortable about the idea of doing something so underhanded and plainly malicious. But I was also aware of the effect Andrew was having on the band, the van, and even the audience members who would approach him after the show and almost instantly back out of the room. And me. It was becoming necessary to find alternate routes through the tiny clubs just to avoid the toxic microclimate that swirled around him after a show.

I did ask why the band didn't simply wash it for him. "Put it in a bathtub and let it soak for a while." It seemed like a reasonable compromise.

"We used to do that, but at this point it just won't come clean. No amount of soaking will get rid of that smell."

Andrew is a very affectionate young man. It's one of his many simple charms, and also one of the immediately apparent contradictions. He stands about six and a half feet tall and almost as broad. He is a fucking mountain. The man is huge. The kind of person that can stand like a rock in the middle of a mosh pit and watch people bounce off him like rubber balls off a concrete wall. And he's a mean looking fucker, too. He does nothing to dispel the sense of menace that comes from huge, aggressive looking, young men. His hair is a peculiar bifurcated mohawk and he usually carries a combination of goatee and stubble that make him look like an unkempt street gang member. I honestly worried about the band's choice of him for bass when I first saw him – he looked like he was going to snap at pretty much any minute. That's a common reaction. Many times on the tour I heard some audience member say "that guy scared the crap out of me at first, but when I talked to him it turned out that he's really nice."

Andrew is, indeed, "really nice." He is exceptionally friendly, warm, and welcoming, if you have the confidence to cross the menacing forcefield he projects. There doesn't appear to be any complicated contradictions or internal torments with Andrew. He is refreshingly uncomplicated and undemanding. Of all the band, he is the first to smother people he's just met with a bear hug.

You just put it together, didn't you? No? Let me give you a minute. Think about it. Andrew. Bear Hug. The shirt. Yeah. If you've received one of those sweat-soaked, ammonia-scented hugs then you're probably rushing off to scrub yourself raw just from the mental image. Something really did need to be done about that shirt.

I won't tell you how it happened or who was responsible. I do know, but there's no point in telling. Just suffice to say that over the next 48 hours, various people made various attempts to "lose" the shirt. Finally, the next day at the Camden Underworld in London, Andrew walked into the dressing room before the show to break the news that his gig shirt was nowhere to be found. I braced for the inevitable eruption of rage but it never came. I think he knew that the shirt's days were numbered. He had tortured his band mates just that little bit too much, left them no choice but subterfuge, and now he seemed prepared to accept the consequences.

And again, it's worth pointing out that no one's thoughts turned to revenge. No one wanted payback. It was just their peculiar way of dealing with it. Andrew was passively pushing things too far by not acting on their requests and so the situation was defused. "Defused" is an interesting choice of words, because I can't imagine the permanent damage – physical and psychological – that would have been done to any poor bomb-sniffing mutt that had the misfortune of shoving his snout into Andrew's luggage.

You may have noticed that I talk a lot about dirt, mess, filth, etc, but until now I haven't mentioned smell. You might be thinking that all five of them reeked on a constant basis. But the truth is they didn't. Laundry facilities may have been in short supply, but they were mercifully fastidious about showering and keeping themselves clean. They didn't smell "fresh and clean as a whistle," they just didn't really smell like anything that I can recall. The "gig shirt" notwithstanding.

The trick, I was later told, was to put an open stick of deodorant into the bag with all of one's clothes. It had a "dry cleaning" kind of an effect. As the bag tumbled and jostled around in the general, perpetual mayhem, the body odour and deodorant did silent battle and somehow canceled each other out. It didn't get the clothes clean, but it did leave them smelling acceptable.

I was also quick to note, right off the bat, that they were all in pretty good physical shape. Instead of being bloated from too much beer, too much sitting around, and too much fast food, they were all fit and trim – possibly the healthiest looking that I'd ever seen them. There was no secret to this – they didn't eat a lot, but when they did it was decent food, and they got at least two hours of extremely intense exercise every day. Not even the impressive quantities of alcohol being consumed could put a damper on it.

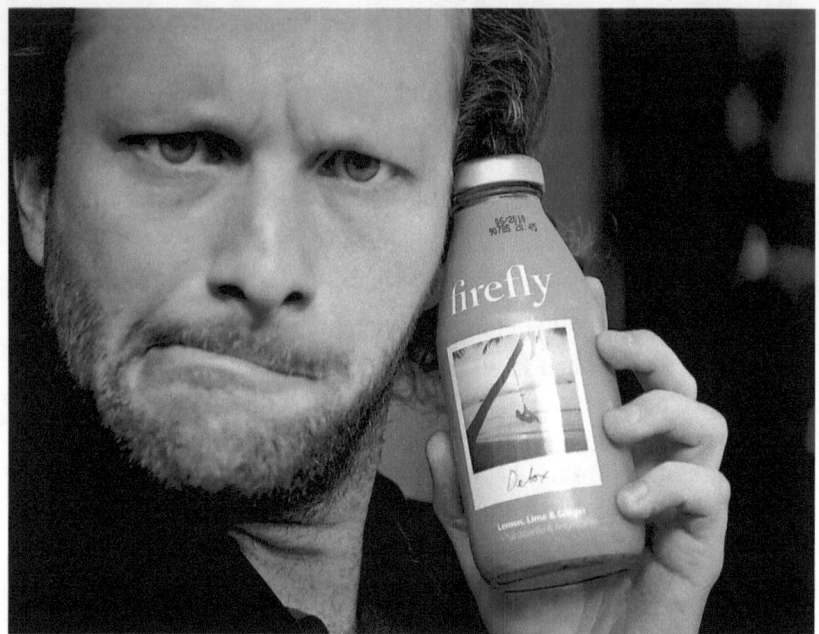

Nick and a bottle of "detox." Needless to say, it didn't work.

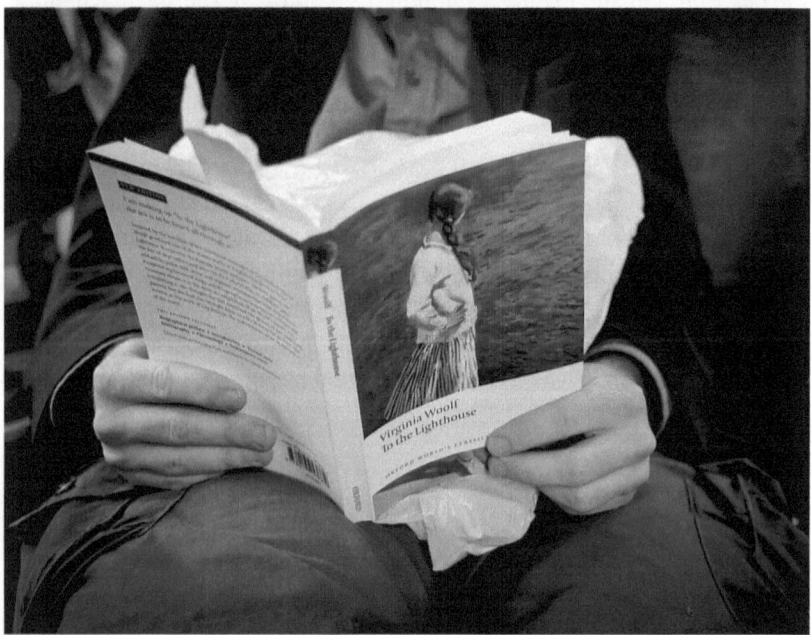

Virginia Woolf – a quiet reminder that the brain trust within the van was, in fact, significant –if carefully hidden most of the time.

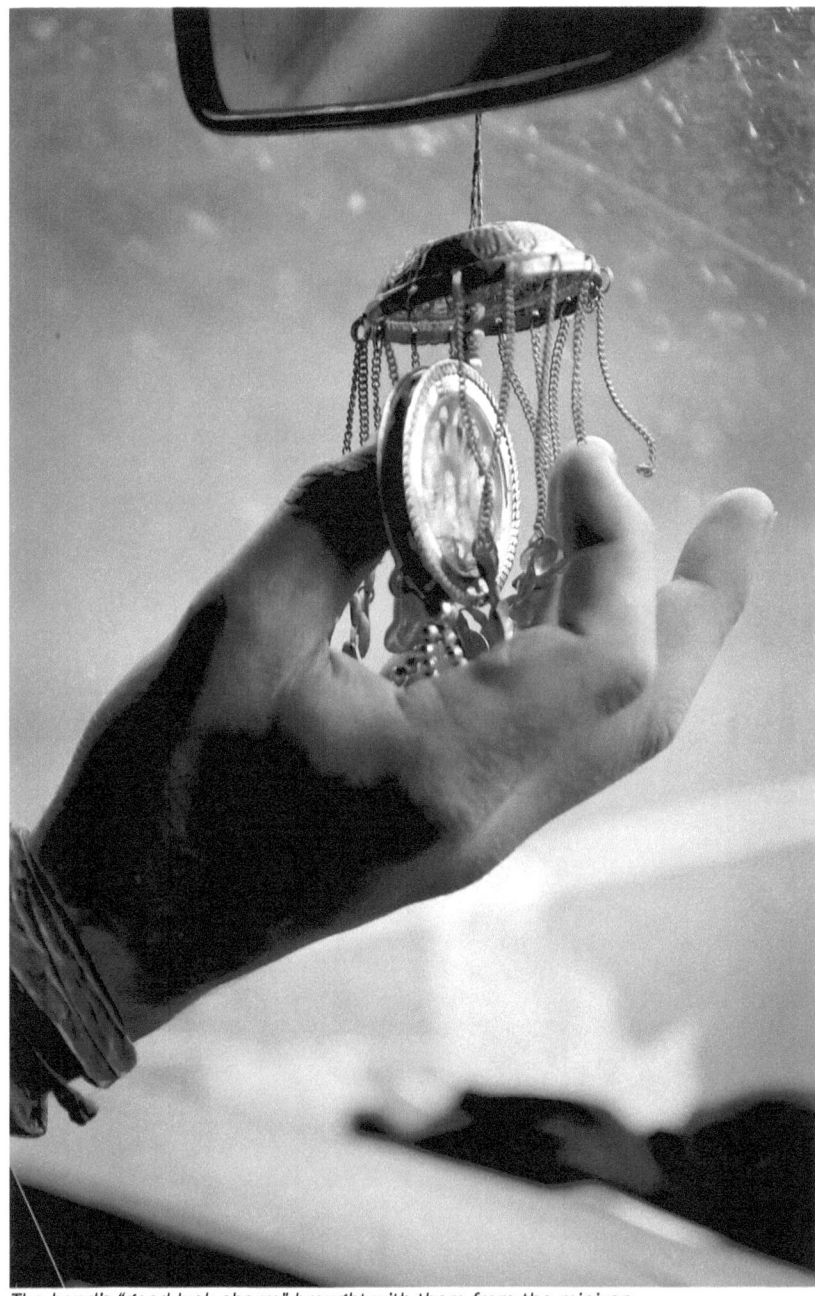

The band's "good luck charm" brought with them from the minivan
they bought in BC. No trip could start without first "tickling" it.

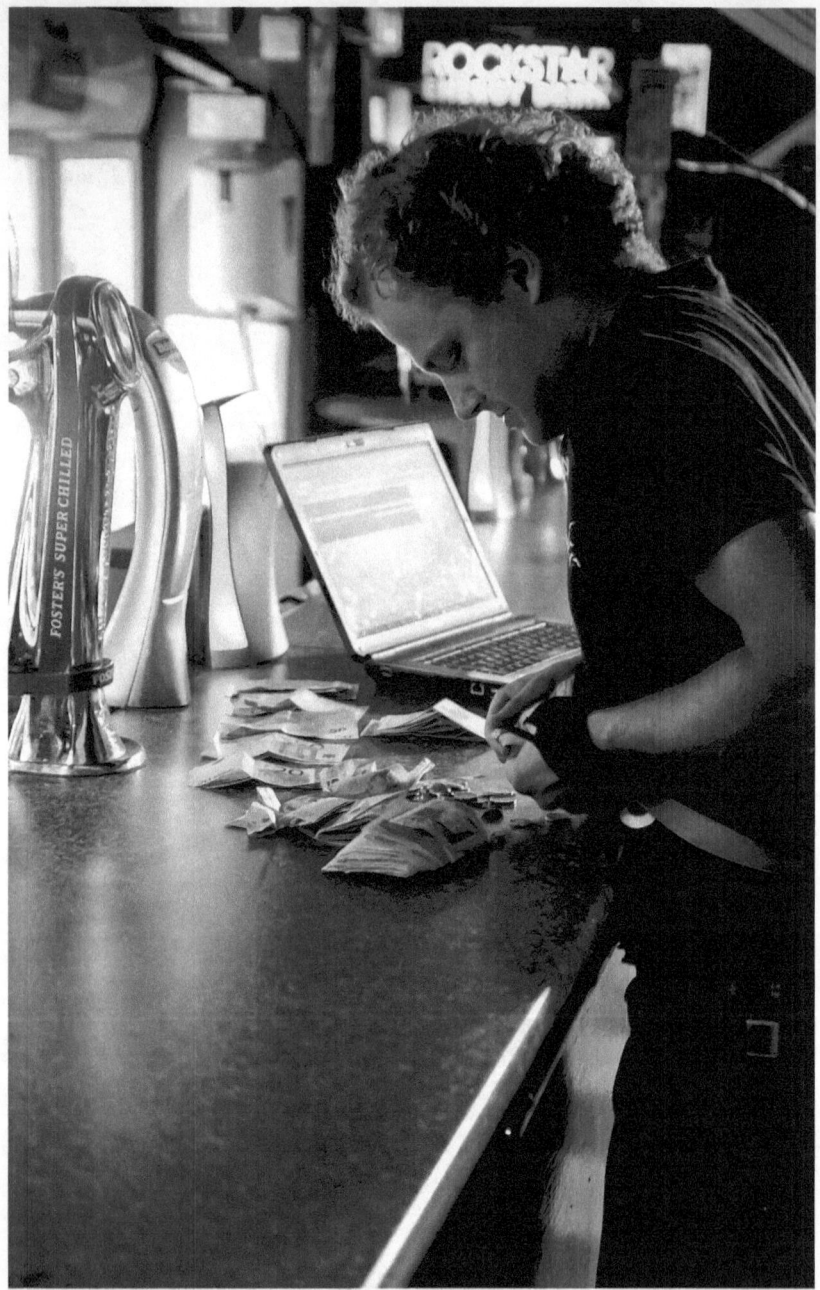

Marco pours the merch proceeds onto the bar for an impromptu bookkeeping session.

This Place Is Awesome

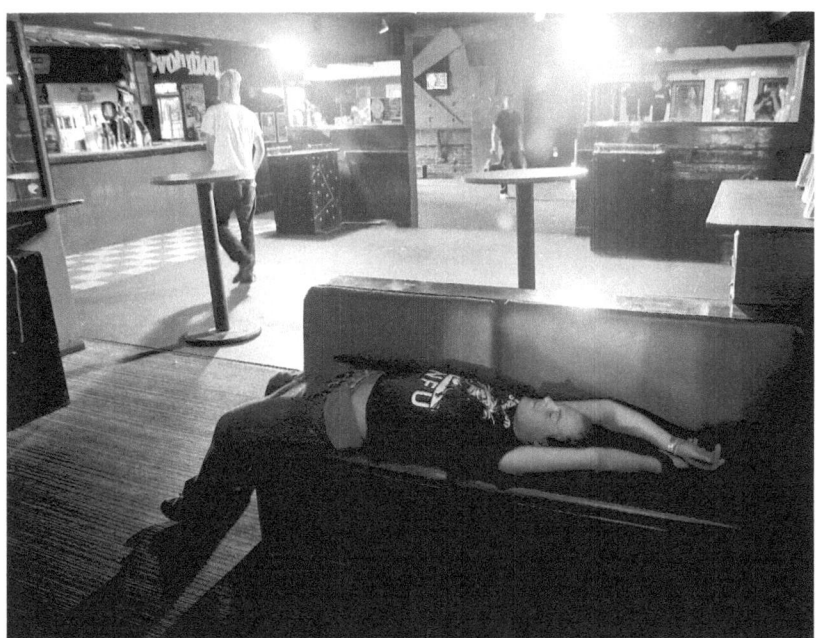

Another opportunity to catch a moment's sleep while waiting for soundcheck in Peterborough. This scene was played out night after night.

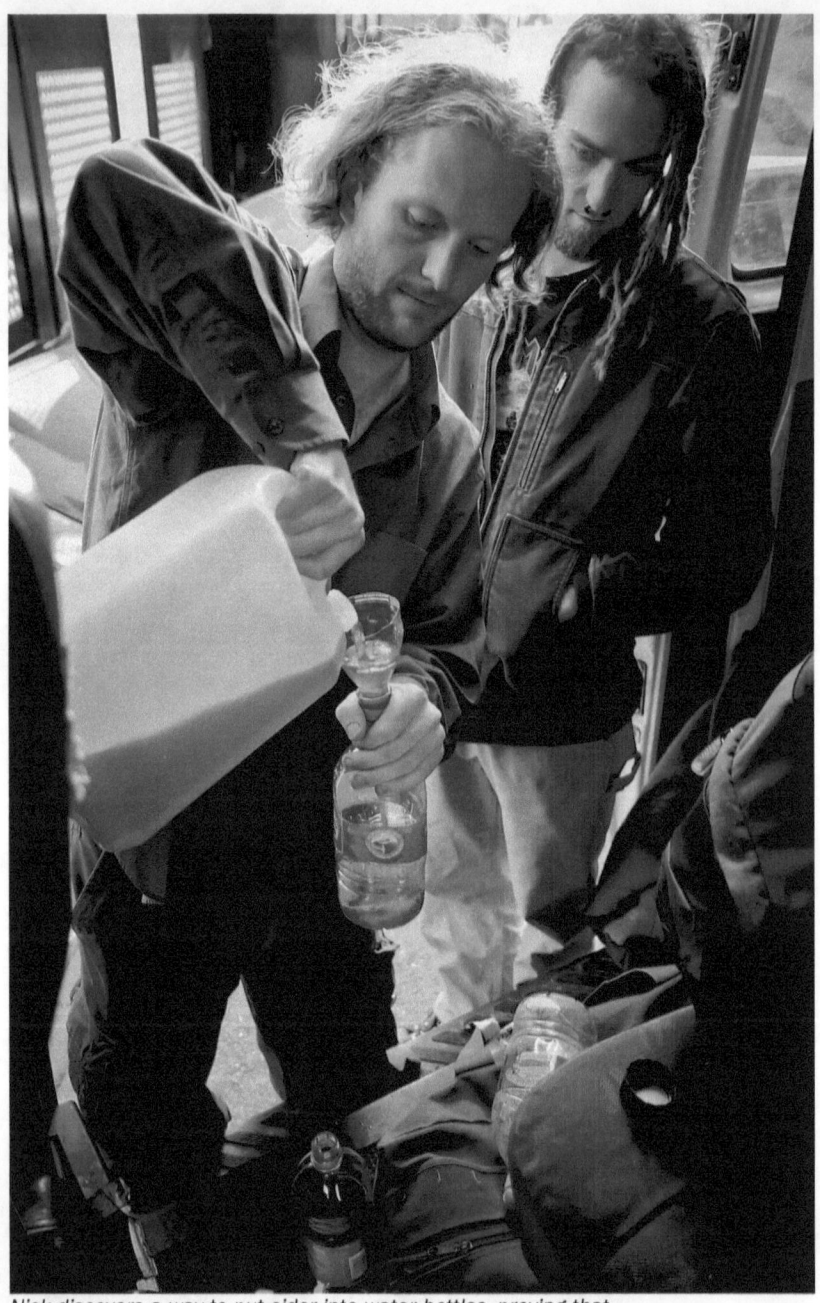

Nick discovers a way to put cider into water bottles, proving that avoiding sobriety is the grandfather of necessity, which is then the mother of invention.

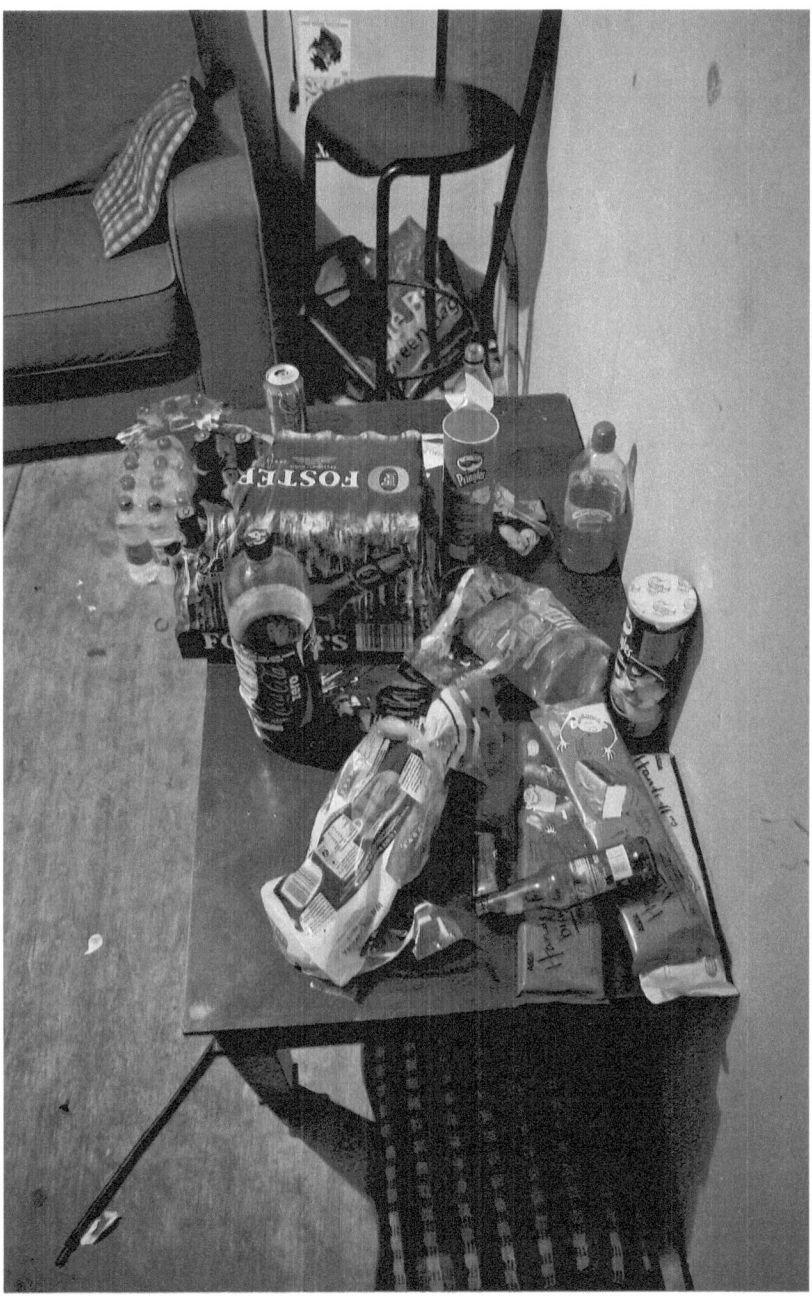

A typical green room - mismatched, dirty furniture, beer, bottled water, and potato chips surrounded by unfinished walls.

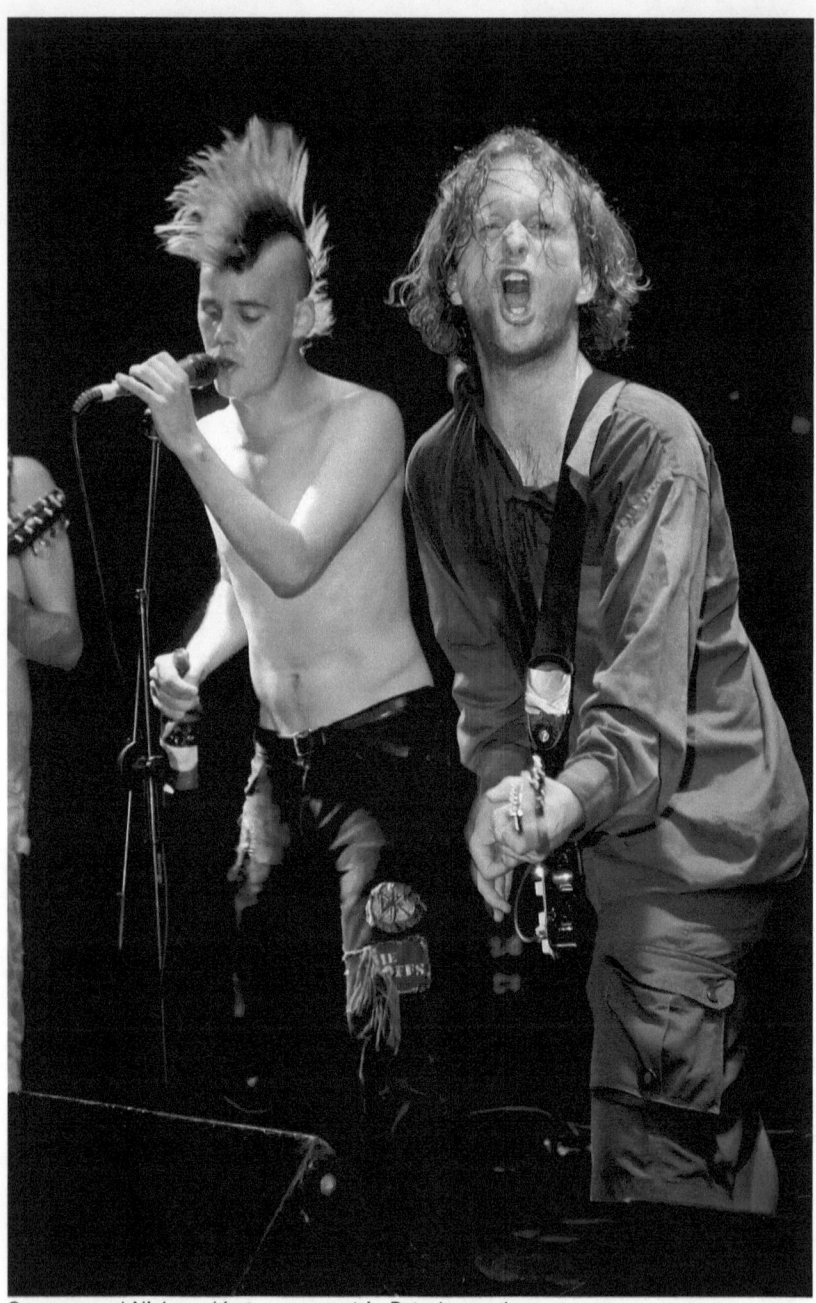

Seamus and Nick working up a sweat in Peterborough.

This Place Is Awesome

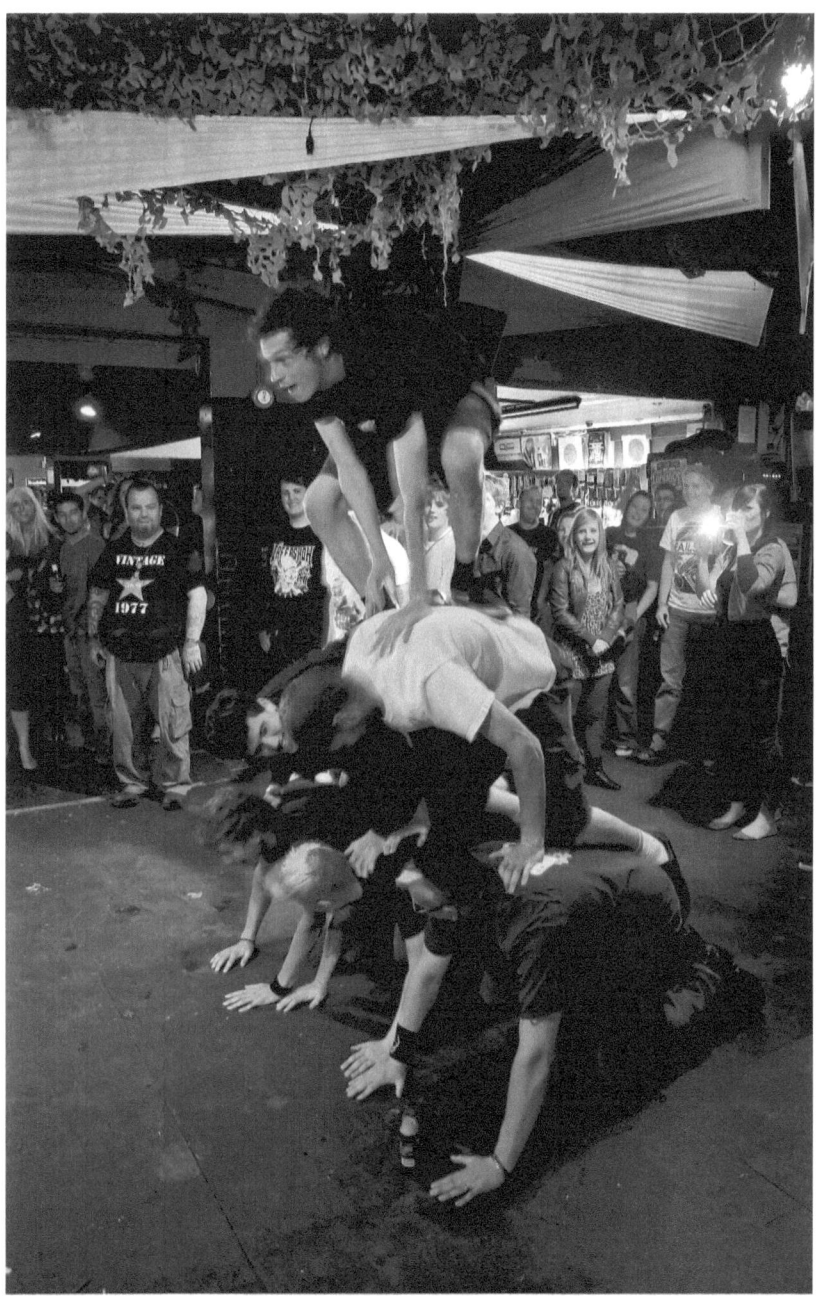

"The pyramid" – one of a number of strange local customs.

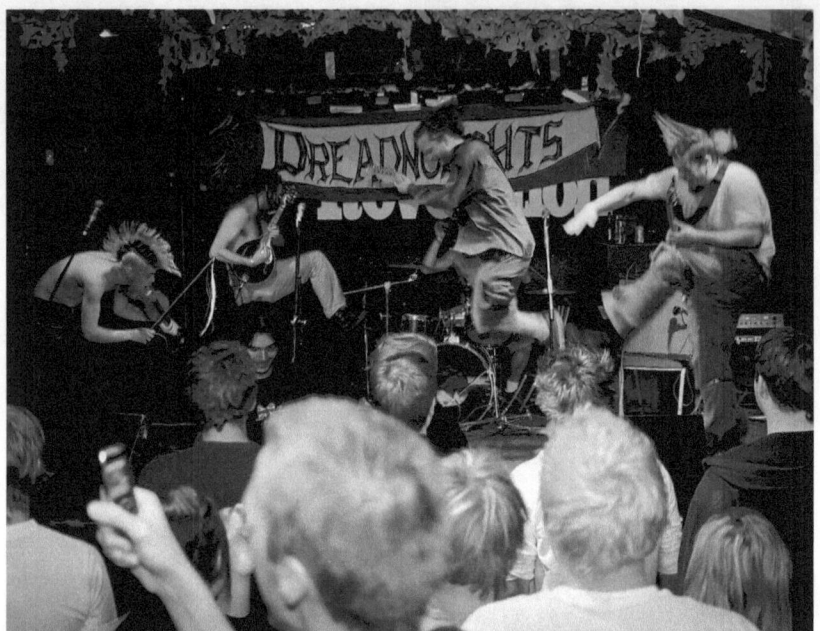

There was always at least one point in every show when all eight feet would leave the ground.

This Place Is Awesome

ALL OVER
BUT THE
SHOWERING.

Day Eight
July 8 – Peterborough, London

The drive to London was uneventful and we located the Camden Underworld, which was beneath the famous World's End pub. According to Wikipedia, it is "rumoured to be" the largest pub in Europe, but the European standard for really big things pales in comparison to North American bigness. We had ample time to kill, so we took to the streets.

Most of the boys had never been to London and Camden is a decent place to land if you're having your first experience there. Like much of London, the unique character of the place is being slowly subverted by chain stores and restaurants, but there's still some cheap, fun rubbish to be found in the open markets and bursting storefronts. The Electric Ballroom continues to operate as a music venue, having seen more changes in musical styles than someone three times the age of the youngest Dreadnought. The whole place is overrun with tourists by day and by night. But it was still miles better than a Monday evening in Stoke.

We wandered around, losing and finding each other again in the various shops and stopping for something to eat by the canal. Then slowly we gravitated back to the World's End, like some giant magnet was pulling us. As we waited for the Underworld's production staff to arrive we milled around the two bars at either ends of the pub. Nick, Seamus, and I, under the spell of a particularly charming bartender, wanted something to drink that we would be unlikely to find anywhere else. "Give us something we've never seen before" we asked, looking at a bewildering array of bottles. The woman offered various types of alcohol that were all pretty pedestrian and familiar, and then pulled out something called Old Krupnik. She said it was what her grandfather drinks back in her home country. It was a disturbing shade of yellow and had a label that looked like it was designed, and possibly printed, before I was born. The booze itself was unremarkable, apart from being sweet, a bit sticky, and that awful shade of yellow. But it has inspired a tradition. Every time The Dreadnoughts come back from some obscure part of Eastern Europe I insist that they bring me back some kind of local booze. I haven't yet received a bottle with nothing but "XXX" on the side, but it's probably just a matter of time. And I'm still hoping that one day I'll have my own bottle of Old Krupnik.

The London gig went well and after the show we poured out onto Camden High Street in search of a place to have a drink. It was time for me to leave the tour and we wanted a quietish place to sit and relax. The strip of Camden we were on seemed to be mostly dance clubs and rowdy venues. Asking the legendary London cab drivers for recommendations didn't get us very far either. So we started walking.

Eventually we found a place that was reasonably quiet and still open for a while, so settled in. We were joined by a prairie ex-pat musician who was living in London for a while. So many of the people you meet on the road are eager to hang around with you, but seem to be unsure of what to do once they get the chance. I've heard stories that Joe Strummer was famous for getting into conversations with local kids at Clash shows, asking them "so what's life like for you here?" He clearly had a knack for engagement. The Dreadnoughts lack that knack. Many times I found myself listening to various band members telling assorted locals about the details of the past couple of days, but rarely did I ever hear them asking questions. This is not a value judgement, but given that opportunity I'd be asking questions about what the local scene is like, how do people live, what do they do, and mostly "what's interesting about this place?" It seemed like such a lost opportunity.

So it was with some relief and pleasure that I found Britanny at the table. Some people have that sharpness in their eyes that lets you know that no matter how much they may be participating in the silly drunken hi-jinx, there's something else going on behind those eyes. Sadly I didn't get much of a chance to talk to her, but being in the presence of someone who hadn't been dulled and demented by life on the road was enough. It was a reminder of what awaited me back in the real world that I'd soon be returning to. I found out later that she somehow located the tour van in the middle of the night and managed to weasel her way into using it as temporary accommodations. In the process, she accidentally pushed Marco over and left him sleeping on top of his drum hardware, which is a bit like trying to sleep on bed of nails but probably not as healthy. I believe she is still apologising for it to this day.

She was not the only stranger at our table though. There was also an odd, middle-aged, blonde woman who was so utterly pissed that she was barely coherent. Of course no one told her to go away, as she stumbled awkwardly into our conversations and generally behaved like she belonged there. The truly rat-arsed and the talented confidence trickster both possess an ability to make everyone feel like their presence is normal and unremarkable. It's the lack of inhibition and steely confidence that leaves everyone else – who is still in possession of a natural social awkwardness – feeling like they'd be acting inappropriately if they were to exclude them. The difference is that the latter will take your money and former will slip off their chair and unexpectedly throw up on your pant leg.

We drank for a couple of hours, walked back to the van which was parked on a quiet side street, and said our goodbyes. We were all a bit tired and numb, so it wasn't a terribly emotional moment. Besides, these boys are a bit unpredictable with their emotions. Just when I think they've forgotten about me, I'll get a drunken, obscene, abusive phone call from some strange part of the Ukraine. In the unmistakeable style of the emotionally retarded, I know that they're saying "we're thinking about you." I wonder what they say to their girlfriends on those same kinds of calls. Then they come back home and forget to tell me that they're doing a show in a weeks' time or that they have a new record out and I find out about it from a stranger.

I took one final picture of the three conscious members standing in front of the van and headed for the bus stop. Two things ran through my mind. Firstly I briefly worried that this photograph may be the last time I saw them alive, knowing how reckless they could be. But reason reasserted itself and I knew the odds, while not impossible, were highly unlikely, and that I'd be seeing them back in Vancouver before too long.

The second thought was my plan for the next hour.

- Get the bus back to the flat were I'd be staying in blissful, quiet, solitude for at least a few days

- Walk straight into the kitchen and get a plastic garbage bag.

- Walk into the shower, put all my clothes into the garbage bag, and have a long hot shower

- Dump the contents of the bag into the clothes dryer. I was staying in a very nice flat in London that was very graciously on loan to me. The idea of bringing bed bugs or some other unwanted visitor in with me was completely unacceptable. Given the squalor and dirt that I'd been living in for the past week, I put the chances at about even.

- Having cleansed myself and my clothes of the physical traces of the tour, the only thing left was to repair the neurological and psychological damage.

And then the final step was not so much part of the plan as an unavoidable inevitability — I collapsed on the couch.

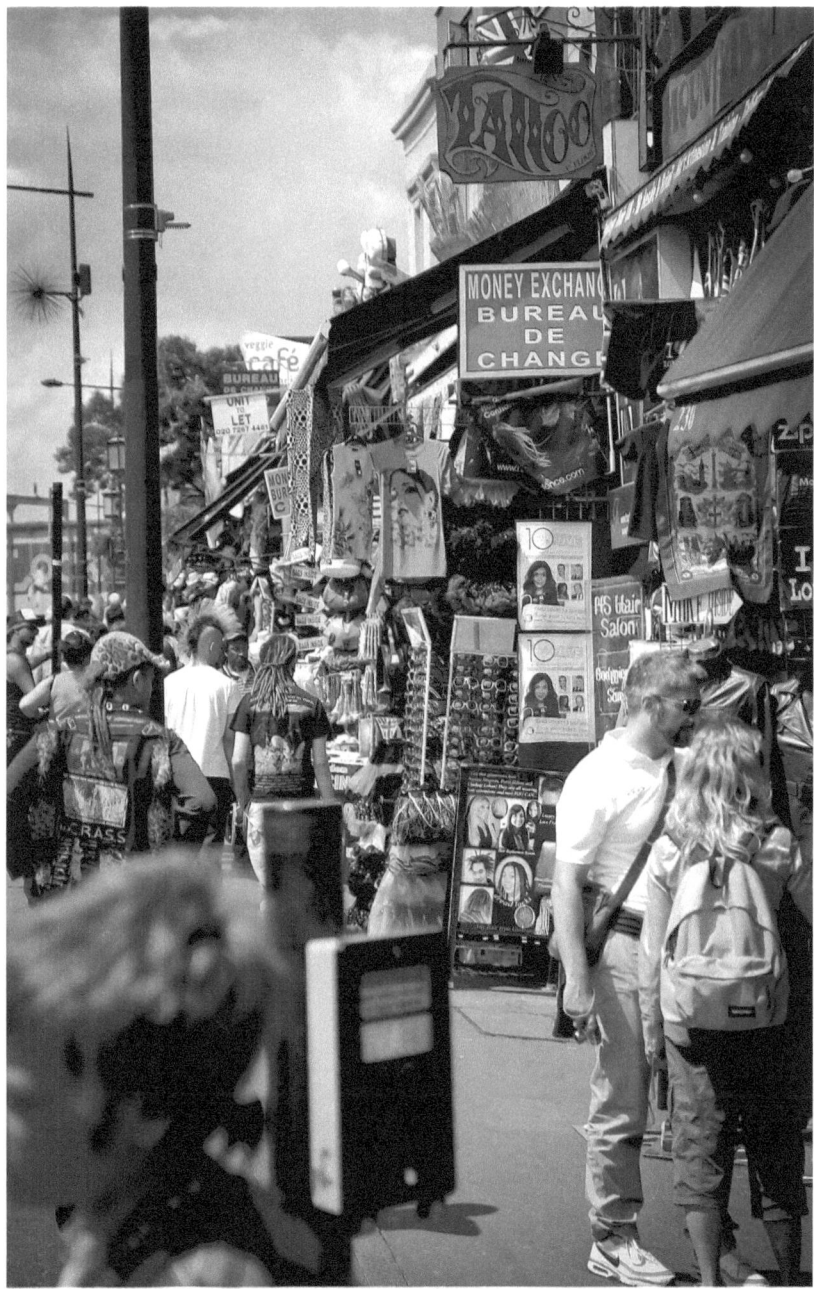

Seamus and Drew lose themselves briefly in the Camden Market.

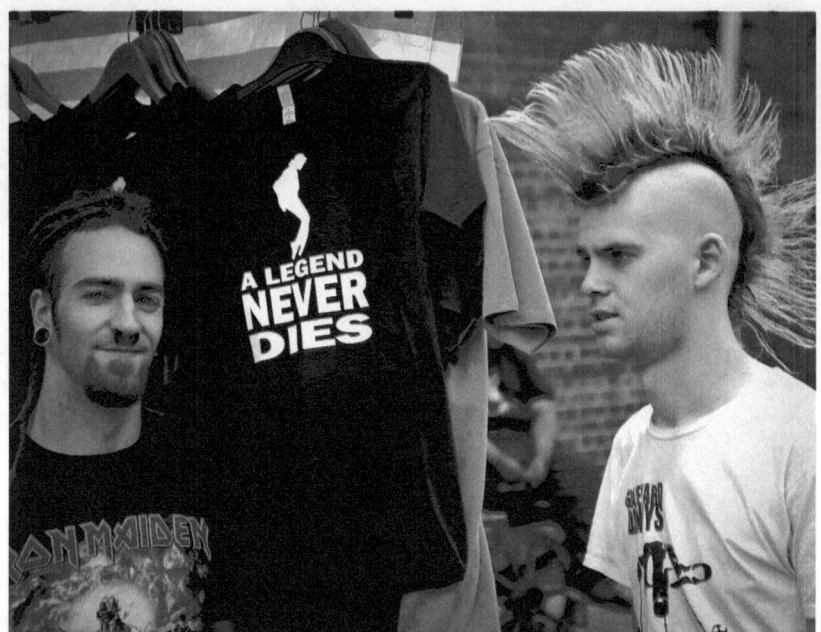

The Dreadnoughts' first CD is called "Legends Never Die", leading to this moment of hysterical irony.

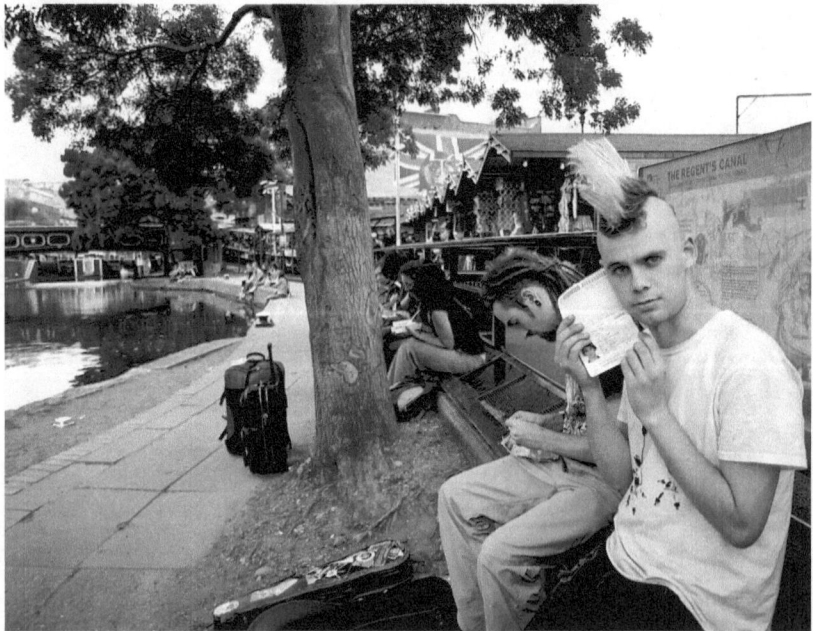

Relaxing for a minute beside the Regent's Canal in Camden Town, London.

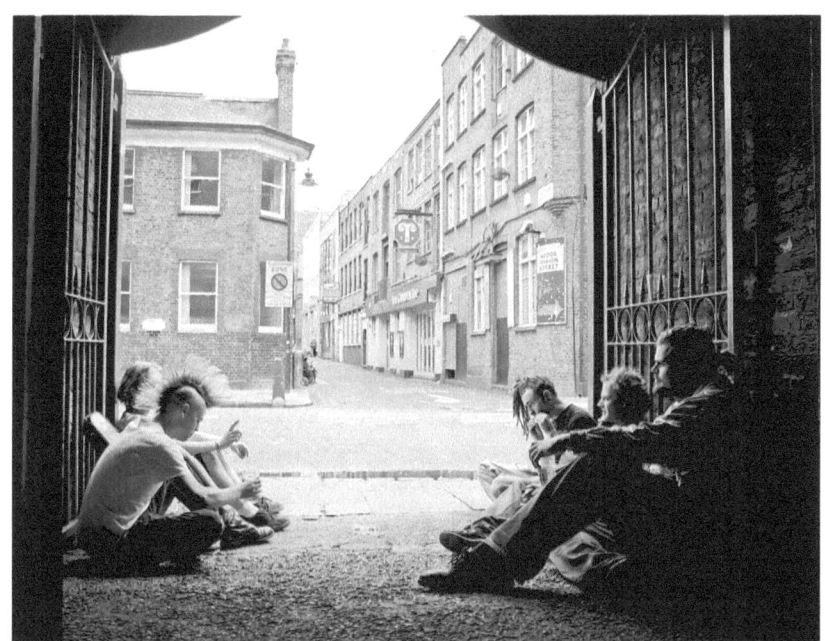

More waiting. Outside the Camden Underworld, London.

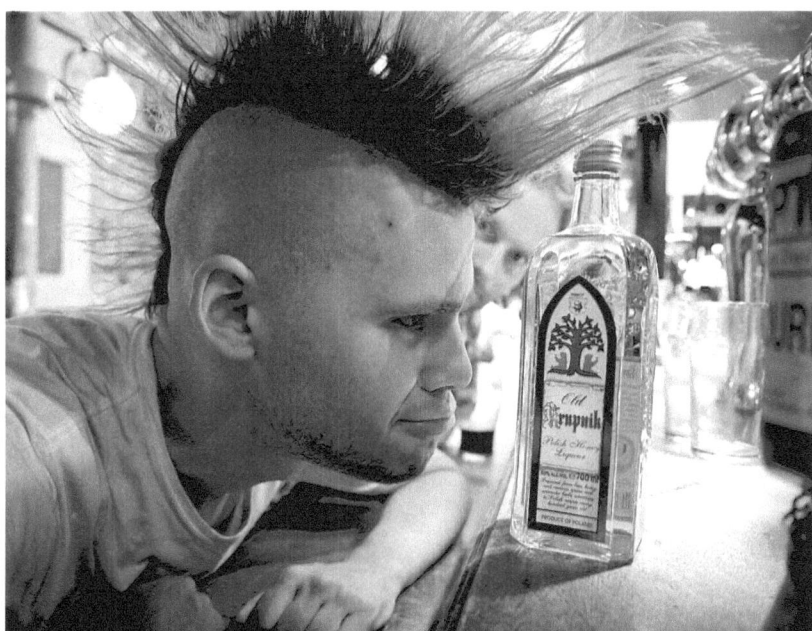

Eager to explore new boozes, we discover "Old Krupnik" – a Polish liqueur that tastes a bit like a bee took a wizz in a bottle of cough syrup – at the Camden Underworld.

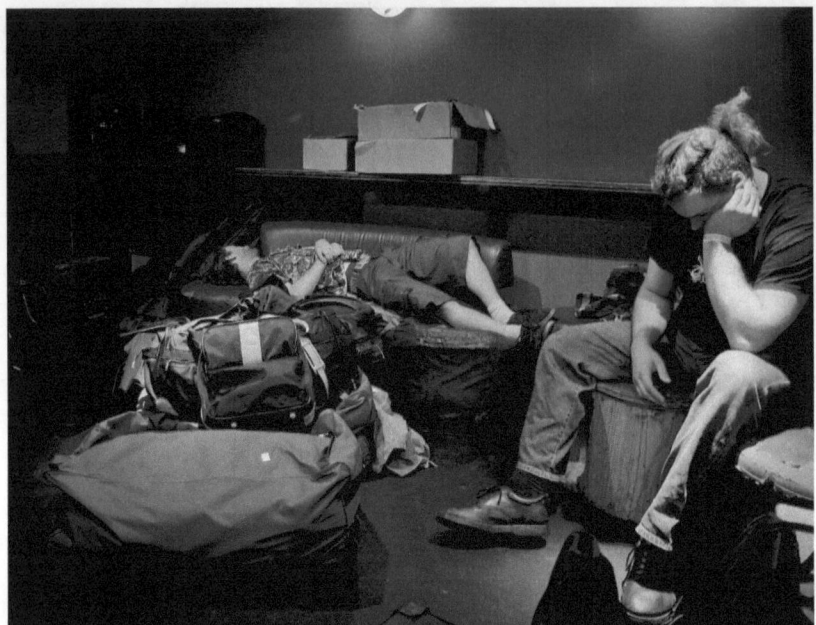

Most people would be surprised to know how much of being a touring band is spent in this condition – not partying or sightseeing, just waiting in dimly lit rooms. Waiting to setup, waiting to sound check, waiting to play, waiting to load out.

This Place Is Awesome

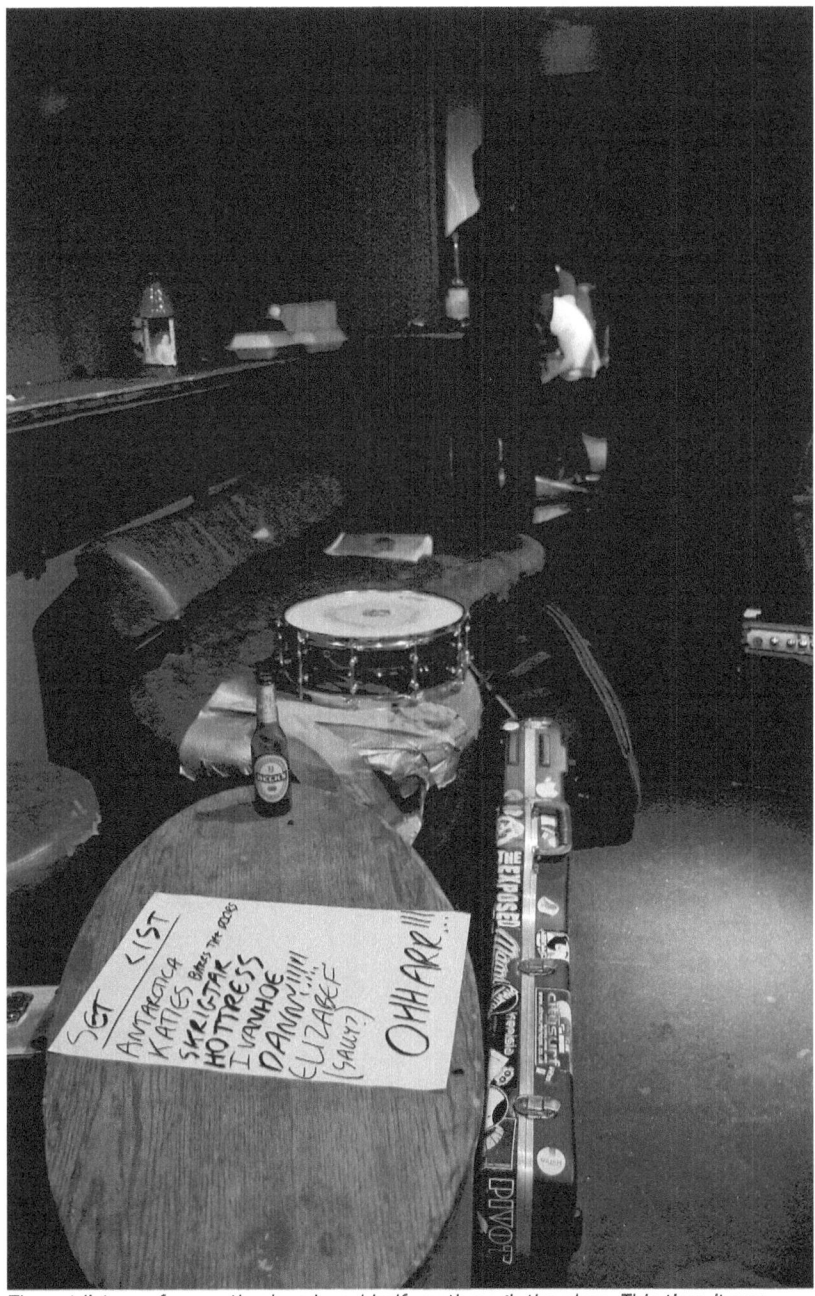

The set list was frequently abandoned halfway through the show. This time it was abandoned before it even got out of the green room.

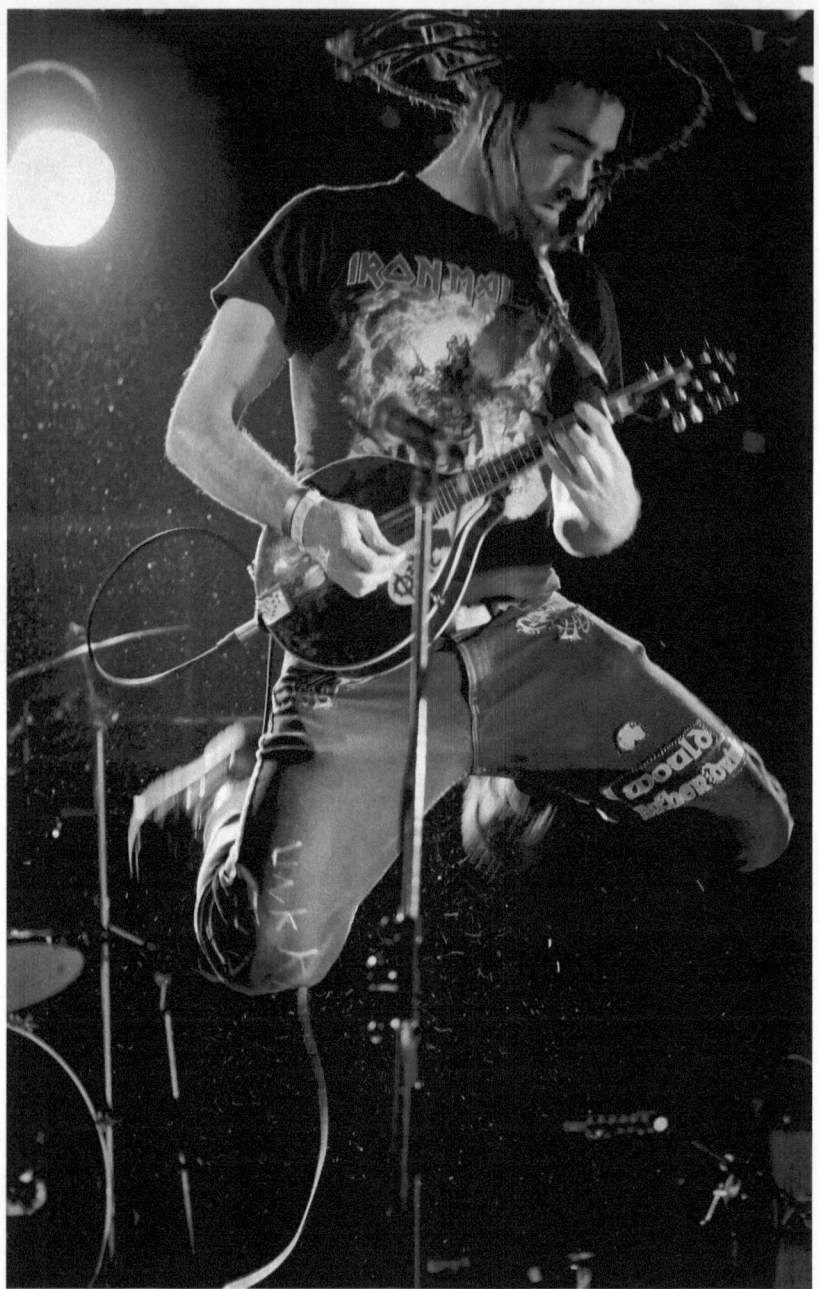

Drew takes flight during The Skrigjaargen Polka.

This Place Is Awesome

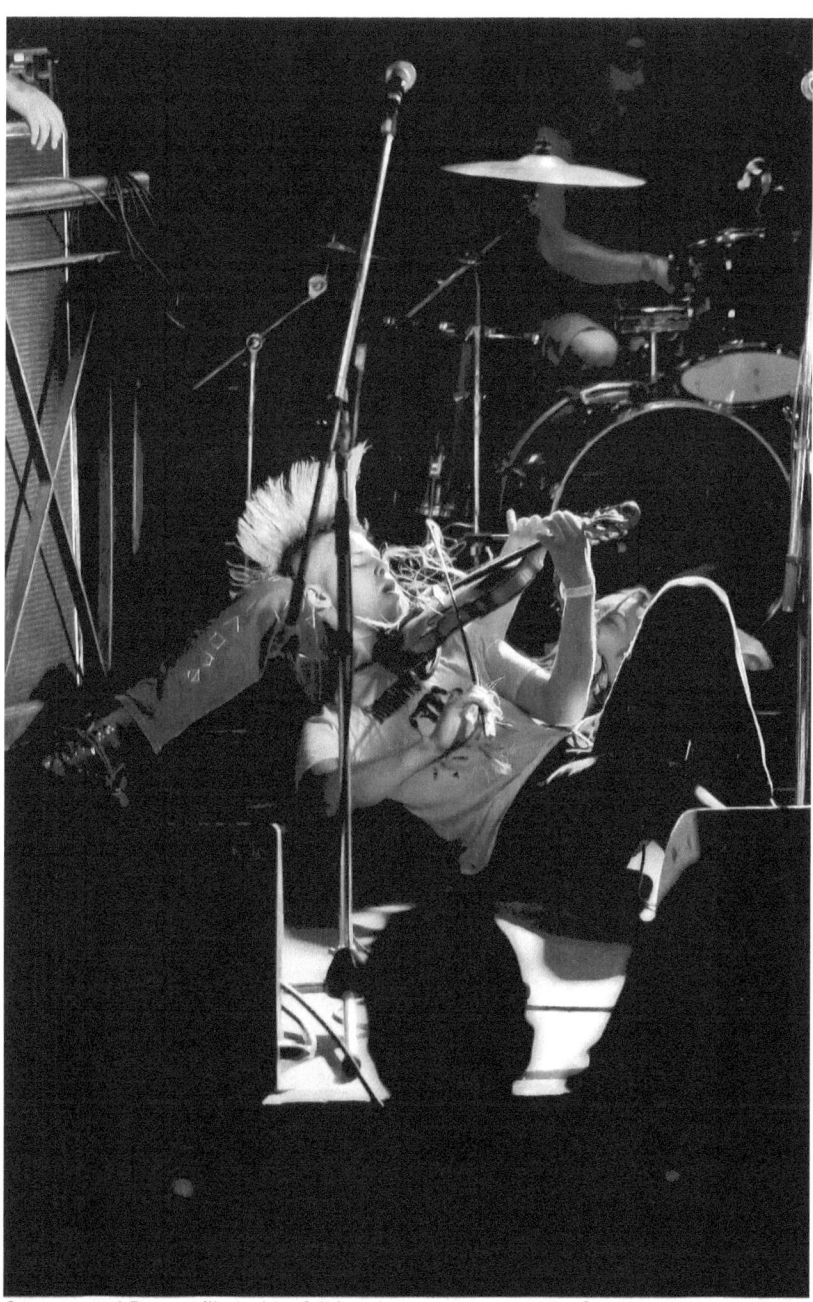

Seamus and Drew, still playing, fall in a heap on stage at the Camden Underworld.

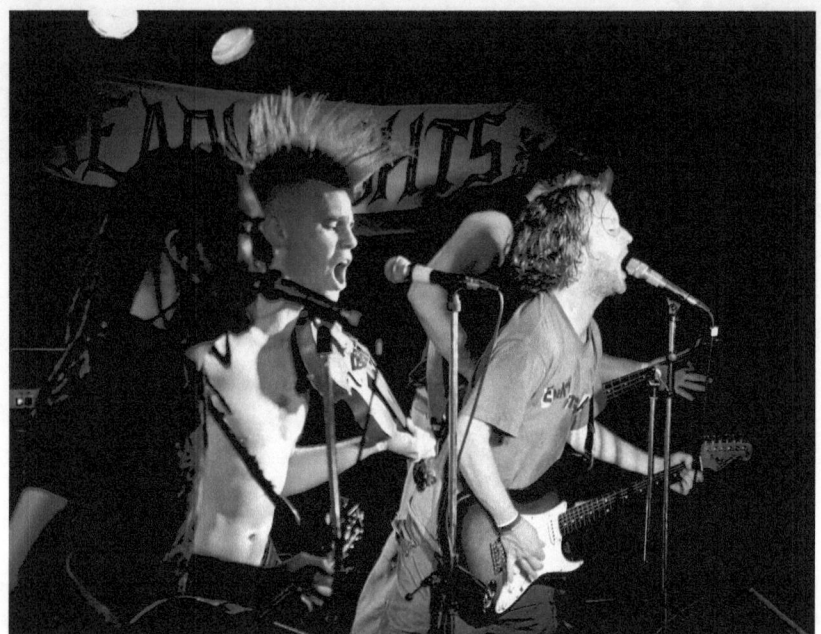

Sweet harmonies at the Camden Underworld.

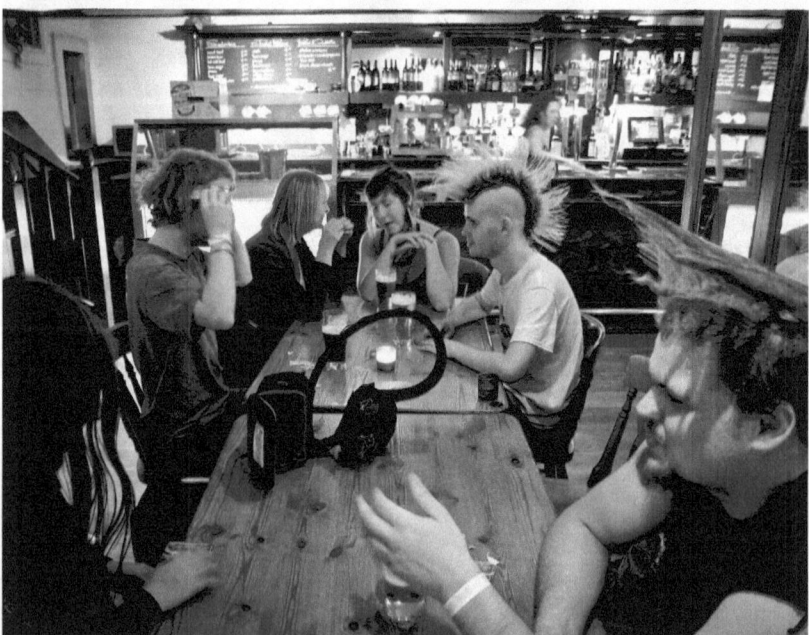

One last drink with an ex-pat Canadian and various drunken interlopers.

This Place Is Awesome

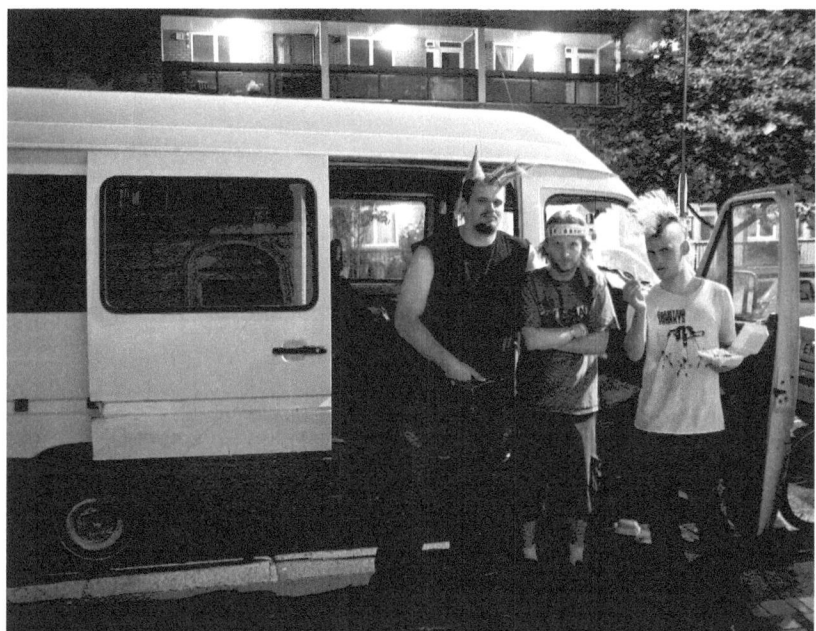

The last I'd see of the boys until a month later when we were all home from our adventures.

This Place Is Awesome

THE RECOVERY.

December 2010

I returned to London on a Sunday and I was scheduled to give a talk about music photography the following Thursday. My wife would also be arriving in London on Thursday. I was extremely grateful for three days of solitude with a task to distract me.

A quick read over my notes made me realise that they could never see the light of day in their raw form. They were too full of criticisms and indictments of the boys' behaviour. It wasn't mean, but it was a bit damning and depressing. It took me quite a while to make sense of it all. I knew that I still liked them all, I just couldn't completely understand why.

Insight, courtesy, thoughtfulness – these things are not rewarded in that environment. The gig was the thing. God help any of them if they were not in condition to perform for the audience, but beyond that there were no expectations and precious little comfort to be found. This was Maslow's pyramid of needs at the broad base – survival. In hindsight I gradually found myself feeling sympathetic towards them and their condition as my distance and objectivity returned. They made a world where life would be difficult and then tried to figure out how to survive there without killing each other or themselves. As I looked at their behaviour in context it made more sense, and I was also able to see the little hints into their true natures that would emerge from time to time.

Literature is full of stories of young people throwing caution and convention out the window, and heading out into the world for an adventure, content to simply see what fate brings them. This was The Dreadnoughts' version of Holden Caulfield, Huckleberry Finn, and Jim

Carroll, but without the hookers, racism, or basketball and heroin, respectively.

As I said earlier, these guys are not natural-born fuck-ups, they just play with it. The appeal is obvious, even to someone like me. The rewards they get while on the road may be small, but the expectations made of them are almost imperceptible. As time sees the tattered clothing either get washed back into acceptability, or simply disintegrate into the ground, the exhaustion and boredom will also slip into the memory hole and what's left will be a series of anecdotes and memories. These will either become the happy memories of a misspent youth, or be embellished and become part of rock and roll history, depending on whether The Dreadnoughts fade into obscurity, or find a measure of success.

One thing I will say about this bunch, they were giving it a serious and energetic try. At that stage of a band's life there is no substitute for sheer bloody-minded determination and indefatigable spirit. They had that in spades, and their willingness to forgo comfort and simplicity in an attempt to see how far their band would go is impressive. This band took the DIY ethic to heart – there was no roadie, no tour bus with DVD players, no managers, no publicists or stylists. If something needed to be carried, they carried it. If it's possible to make a name for yourself based solely on effort and talent, then these guys deserve it.

APWS

This Place Is Awesome

ABOUT THE AUTHOR.

Adam PW Smith was 43 years old when he started a week of touring around Britain with The Dreadnoughts. He was 87 years old by the time that week was over.

Adam has been involved with the Canadian independent music scene from the time he was old enough to hoist a Fender amp into the back of a Ford Econoline van. He started out taking live music photographs of bands like The Cult, Sex Gang Children, and Deja Voodoo in the early 1980s. After a long hiatus from photography he got back into it in 2000 and has been intensely photographing parts of the Vancouver independent music scene for the past five years, as well as shooting events in the United States and Britain. His photographs have appeared in the Georgia Straight, Guitar Player Magazine, Seattle Weekly, SF Weekly, The Globe and Mail, and countless daily newspapers around the world, and have been featured on the BBC and CBC Web sites. More importantly to him, his photographs are a familiar sight on the Myspace, Facebook, and Web site pages of many of Vancouver's best live indie bands.

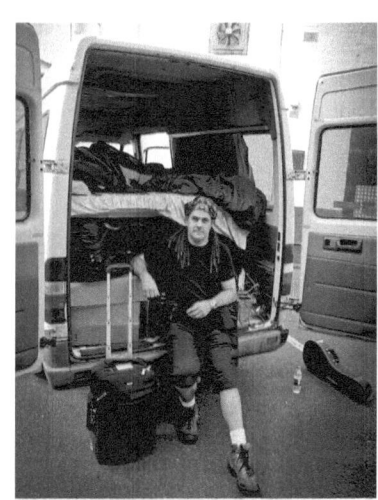

Peterborough 2009

Champion of the musical underdog, lover of gin, and award-winning bad poet, he values music, integrity, and respect over money. Which is good, because that's order in which those things are to be found in his life.

This Place Is Awesome

Adam PW Smith █ Photography

Web: www.adampwsmith.com
Email: adam@adampwsmith.com
Facebook: www.facebook.com/adampwsmithphotography
           www.facebook.com/ThisPlaceIsAwesome
Twitter: @adampwsmith

A Dreadnoughts music video, directed and shot by Adam PW Smith and featuring live footage from their 2011 European tour, can be found at:

www.youtube.com/user/taktaktakfilms/

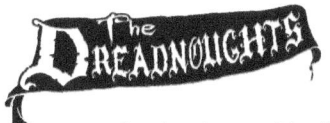

www.facebook.com/thedreadnoughts

www.myspace.com/vancitydreadnoughts

www.thedreadnoughts.com

The Dreadnoughts have five CDs:

Legends Never Die

Victory Square

Cider Punks Unite

Polka's Not Dead

Uncle Touchy Goes To College

They are available through the iTunes Music Store and better independent record shops.

www.ingramcontent.com/pod-product-compliance
Lightning Source LLC
Chambersburg PA
CBHW032025170526
45157CB00002B/856